DAFFODILS
For Home, Garden and Show

Don Barnes

DAFFODILS

For Home, Garden and Show

DAVID & CHARLES
Newton Abbot   London

TO
CAROL, IRENE AND
A DEAR MOTHER

Title page
OVER ONE HUNDRED YEARS of breeding work have changed the shape and colouring of daffodils. The centre bloom is Barri *conspicuus* (3Y-YYR), registered in 1884 and hailed as a wonderful development. The narrow, twisted perianth and the colouring are far removed from present-day red and yellow cultivars. The surrounding flowers are: (top left) Torridon (2Y-R); (top right) Liverpool Festival (2Y-O); (bottom left) Loch Hope (2Y-R); and (bottom right) Achduart (3Y-R)

British Library Cataloguing in Publication Data

Barnes, Don
  Daffodils: for home, garden and show.
  1. Daffodils
  I. Title
  635.9'3425   SB413.D12

  ISBN 0–7153–8853–3

Typeset by ABM Typographics Limited, Hull
and printed in Great Britain
by Butler & Tanner Limited, Frome and London
for David & Charles Publishers plc
Brunel House   Newton Abbot   Devon

Contents

Introduction

Daffodils are well-loved flowers that make a welcome sight each spring. They survive the worst of the weather that winter provides and come smiling through to bless our gardens with splashes of colour that brighten even the dullest of days.

Convention implies that daffodils must be yellow and, indeed, many are available in delightful golden tones. However, over the last one hundred years or so the dedicated work of many breeders has resulted in a whole range of colours to complement the yellows: pinks, oranges, reds and whites now add sparkling variety to this popular genus. But you may say 'it is the narcissus that has the white petals and not the daffodil'. The name 'narcissus' has been commonly used to describe daffodils with white petals, but white and yellow flowers interbreed quite happily and produce offspring in both colours. So they are the same family, or genus, which botanically is named Narcissus and which has been familiarly known as the daffodil; the names are interchangeable.

The various colours of the daffodil create hundreds of different flowers; and as if that is insufficient, the family has a number of different sizes and forms, or styles. Some wonderfully attractive blooms have broad petals, up to 4½in (12cm) in diameter, and the characteristic large trumpet. At the other end of the scale are some of the species, with flowers not more than ½in (1cm) in diameter, which are perfect miniature versions of their larger brothers and sisters. A very high proportion of daffodils produce only one flower to each stem but even these single-headed beauties can have trumpets, large cups or small cups; they can have disproportionately small petals, as in the bulbocodiums, or swept-back petals as in the cyclamineus hybrids. The range of possibilities is almost limitless. Others carry a number of flower-heads on each stem. Some consistently produce two or three per stem and others, with good cultivation, achieve in excess of twenty delicate heads with the single stem appearing to support a tiny bunch of colour. The wide range of cultivars, in excess of 20,000 have been given names registered with the Royal Horticultural Society, means that something is available for most uses, whether in the garden, the window box, the rock garden or even hanging baskets. Indeed, a very versatile subject.

Because of the range and the breeding back to species, the time of flowering is also quite varied. Traditionally, we associate daffodils with spring, when the majority do give their best displays over a period of about six weeks; but there are some which extend the time-scale almost through to summer. A limited number flower in the autumn and some come to perfection in winter. For at least six months of the year, daffodils can be in flower at their naturally determined dates and in a recurring sequence. Manipulation of the natural flowering dates is possible, without too much difficulty, and this makes the daffodil a very useful subject for home decoration. Indeed, most florists have daffodils available for over six months, using imported and home-raised blooms, both forced and natural.

Daffodils are remarkably trouble-free in the garden and can and do remain healthy for many years. Their good health, tolerance and resilience make them ideal for naturalising in massed displays. It can also, regrettably, count against them as it is often assumed that they thrive on neglect. Attention to some basic cultural principles is certain to be repaid with more abundant blooms.

Newly introduced daffodil cultivars rarely get the same favourable publicity afforded to, say, a new rose, chrysanthemum or sweet-pea. However, high prices do attract publicity and some of the rarer colour breaks can change hands for over £100 (US $150) for a single bulb. This is not a new phenomenon — three bulbs of Will Scarlet changed hands in 1899 for £100. Fortune,

now sold by the hundreds of tons each year, was introduced in 1923 and sold for £50 (US $75) per bulb and maintained high prices for a very long time. Fortunately there are hundreds of different cultivars available at prices similar to those applicable to annual bedding plants. Each bulb, with reasonable treatment, represents a real investment and will bloom year after year and multiply fairly rapidly.

Daffodils are unlikely to lose their popularity as harbingers of spring. Breathtaking massed plantings are always memorable and can still be seen, and even the smallest of modern gardens can be brilliantly enhanced by a clump of daffodils in a border. In the home, daffodils can be used to create colourful flower arrangements suitable for many occasions, and grown in pots and decorative containers give super long-lasting displays. Some delightful cultivars have a bonus of distinctive perfumes.

Daffodils provide so many opportunities for the average gardener that they must be regarded as indispensable. An individual bloom has a refinement of form and precision that is rarely equalled and for the competitively-minded the genus is ideal for exhibitions in the spring.

The information in the following chapters will perhaps encourage you to try some new cultivars in addition to your 'tried and tested' favourites, and will at least help you to get the maximum enjoyment from daffodils.

A SUPER BLOOM of Dailmanach (2W-P) showing the perfection in detail that makes it a consistently successful show cultivar. It was the first pink to be awarded the title of overall Best Bloom at a Royal Horticultural Society show (1972). Its growth and substance are such that it will be popular for many years and ultimately for garden display

•1•
Flower Structure and Classification

How fortunate we are that daffodils have been given so much attention by breeders. Every year dozens of new beauties are added to the International Register and there are no signs that this will end. New and exciting breaks of colour and form are still emerging, so that for sheer variety the genus has much to offer every gardener.

The word 'daffodil' brings to mind a particular spring flower both in terms of shape and colour. A large proportion of daffodils do produce their flowers in the spring but there are some that naturally bloom in the autumn, winter or early summer. Many years ago most daffodils were in shades of yellow; the range of colours now available includes whites, oranges, reds and pinks and various combinations but does not extend to blues and purples, and only rarely is green colouring present in the bloom. The traditional wide-mouth trumpet of the daffodil is still popular though many different shapes have been developed. The majority of daffodils have only one flower per stem but there are many hundreds that produce a small bunch of flowers on each stem.

The daffodil flower is essentially a simple structure, although variations of shape, proportion, colour and number of heads may give a false impression of complexity. Among the thousands of known daffodils some cultivars or species have characteristics which cannot be adequately embraced by the standard descriptions. Such exceptions do not invalidate the descriptions but do establish the point that we are trying to produce an order out of an infinite number of variables. Nature does not know that it must conform to man-made systems, which in any event can be no more than workable generalisations. The basic parts of the daffodil, and their functions, are explained in Fig 1.

Recognising that these are the basic parts of any daffodil flower it is the combinations of these few variables that give rise to the vast range of cultivars which now exist. Petals can range from the very narrow remnants found in *Narcissus bulbocodium* through to the immensely broad segments favoured for exhibition blooms such as Burntollet and Gold Convention. The corona varies from the wide-mouthed cylinder of the trumpet daffodils and *N cyclamineus* to the minute collars of the poeticus group, the laid-back lobes of the 'split-coronas', and the host of petaloids of the double daffodils. Combine these variations with different colours and it is easy to see how a whole range of daffodils has been created and the options that can still be pursued.

CLASSIFICATION

To assist in the description of the known daffodils there have been various attempts to establish standard classifications. In all cases the different systems have related the hybrids (cultivars) to the typical species, except for the larger flowers where relative relationships between length of perianth and corona have been used to create the 'Divisions'. The Victorians named these Divisions to honour the pioneer daffodil breeders whereas now we simply rely upon numbers and secondary descriptions. Modern technology has enabled the classification system to be computerised: developed by Dr Tom Throckmorton, the now universally adopted system of 'colour coding' uses numbers to describe the type of the flower by reference to the Divisions and letters to signify the major colours found in each part of the flower. For example, an all yellow trumpet daffodil is classified as 1Y-Y, a bicolour trumpet daffodil with white perianth and yellow corona as 1W-Y and a double daffodil with yellow petals and an intermix of red petaloids as 4Y-R. The system is detailed in full in Appendix I and within its limitations it gives a readily understood idea of each cultivar; however, it cannot give any real indication as to the size to be expected of each bloom or the length of the stem, or indeed of any other characteristic. These other variables have been recorded by Dr Throckmorton and are available as a computer print-out through the American Daffodil Society, providing a simple picture for comparison. The system is a useful guide for daffodil growers though it has its faults, which largely arise from incorrect descriptions at the time of registration.

The fundamental definitions of the classification system have been in use since 1950. There are twelve recognised Divisions of daffodils which generally rely upon the appearance of the flowers.

Divisions 1, 2 and 3 all have only one flower to each stem and are hybrids of garden origin. Visual comparison of the relative lengths of corona and perianth segment are not sufficiently reliable and a rule must be used. The measurements are taken from the junction of corona and perianth along the midrib of the outer perianth segment to its extreme tip, and from the same point along the outside of the corona to its furthest extension, with any roll or frill being flattened out. There is no particular convention about the use of imperial or metric units for measurement but accuracy is essential.

Many people believe the Division 6 flowers should retain a gracefulness of form and size to avoid looking like badly-reflexed Division 1, 2 or 3 blooms. The smaller flowers, such as Dove Wings (6W-Y) and Lilac Charm (6W-GPP), are perhaps the finest examples of this Division and clearly retain the true characteristics of the species.

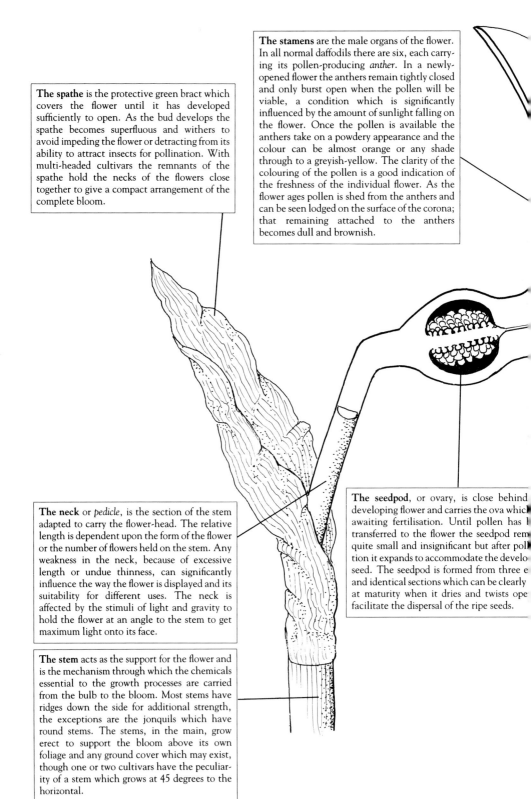

The spathe is the protective green bract which covers the flower until it has developed sufficiently to open. As the bud develops the spathe becomes superfluous and withers to avoid impeding the flower or detracting from its ability to attract insects for pollination. With multi-headed cultivars the remnants of the spathe hold the necks of the flowers close together to give a compact arrangement of the complete bloom.

The stamens are the male organs of the flower. In all normal daffodils there are six, each carrying its pollen-producing *anther*. In a newly-opened flower the anthers remain tightly closed and only burst open when the pollen will be viable, a condition which is significantly influenced by the amount of sunlight falling on the flower. Once the pollen is available the anthers take on a powdery appearance and the colour can be almost orange or any shade through to a greyish-yellow. The clarity of the colouring of the pollen is a good indication of the freshness of the individual flower. As the flower ages pollen is shed from the anthers and can be seen lodged on the surface of the corona; that remaining attached to the anthers becomes dull and brownish.

The neck or *pedicle*, is the section of the stem adapted to carry the flower-head. The relative length is dependent upon the form of the flower or the number of flowers held on the stem. Any weakness in the neck, because of excessive length or undue thinness, can significantly influence the way the flower is displayed and its suitability for different uses. The neck is affected by the stimuli of light and gravity to hold the flower at an angle to the stem to get maximum light onto its face.

The seedpod, or ovary, is close behind developing flower and carries the ova which awaiting fertilisation. Until pollen has transferred to the flower the seedpod rem quite small and insignificant but after poll tion it expands to accommodate the develo seed. The seedpod is formed from three e and identical sections which can be clearly at maturity when it dries and twists ope facilitate the dispersal of the ripe seeds.

The stem acts as the support for the flower and is the mechanism through which the chemicals essential to the growth processes are carried from the bulb to the bloom. Most stems have ridges down the side for additional strength, the exceptions are the jonquils which have round stems. The stems, in the main, grow erect to support the bloom above its own foliage and any ground cover which may exist, though one or two cultivars have the peculiarity of a stem which grows at 45 degrees to the horizontal.

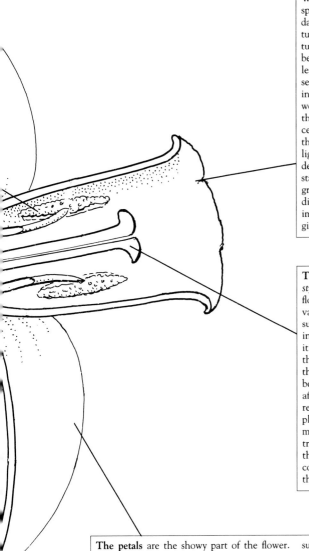

The corona is the central part of the flower. With the exception of the recently developed split-corona daffodils and the doubles, all daffodils have a characteristic single circular tube surrounding the stamens and stigma. This tube, correctly known as the corona, can also be known as the trumpet, where its length is at least as great as the length of the perianth segment, or the cup. The corona can be found in a wide variety of shapes and dimensions as well as many different colours. The majority of the colour pigment, usually carotin B, is concentrated in the corona and hence this part of the flower is most susceptible to damage by sunlight. Although the function of the corona is debatable it does offer protection to the stamens and stigma as well as being a landing ground for insects that occasionally assist in the dispersal of pollen. Certainly the corona is an important part of the flower and one which gives each cultivar its unique appearance.

The stigma is the pollen-receiving tip of the *style*, a stalk-like part of the female organ of the flower. The exact shape and size of the stigma varies considerably but essentially it is a sticky surface with an orifice leading through the style into the seedpod. After the flower has opened it takes some three or four days for the surface of the stigma to become fully receptive and create the fluid which will permit the pollen grains to be transported to the ova. Climatic conditions affect the speed at which the surface becomes receptive and can therefore also affect the plant's ability to set viable seed. The stigma may be displayed above the stamens, as in the trumpet daffodils, or partially concealed by them, as in the cultivars with short flat coronas. The form of the stigma can enhance the appearance of the flower.

The petals are the showy part of the flower. Normally a daffodil has six petals which are collectively known as the *perianth*. The number of petals does vary occasionally but this usually indicates that there has been some damage to the embryo by insects or extremes of temperature and such variations should be regarded as freaks. Double daffodils still retain an outer ring of six petals, or perianth segments, though depending upon the form of the particular cultivar there may appear, upon superficial examination, to be more. The perianth segments are equally spaced around the flower in two layers of three. The larger, outer segments have an arrangement of interlocking hooks which hold the enlarging bud together until it has developed sufficiently and the flower is ready to display itself for pollination. The perianth in a fully-developed flower will normally be held at right angles to the neck, though some cultivars show a tendency to 'hood' over the corona and others a tendency to reflex from the corona as in the cyclamineus types (see page 00). Perianth segments have different shapes and colours which give each cultivar its characteristic form, and current trends are for broad overlapping petals to produce a flower which looks very round. Usually the perianth segments are of a uniform colour, though in some cases they can appear to be stained with colour from the corona or carrying a flush of the same colouring, or to have a halo of lighter colour round the base of the corona.

The following points enlarge upon the official definitions to assist in the recognition of cultivars:

Division 1 Trumpet daffodils. The length of the corona must be at least as great as that of the perianth segments. Often as the bud is opening the rim of the corona is clearly visible extending beyond the perianth.

Division 2 Large-cupped daffodils. The length of the corona is less than that of the perianth but greater than one-third.

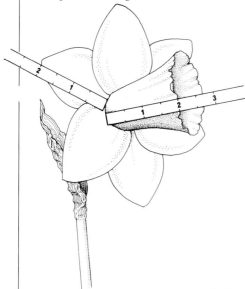

MEASUREMENT OF THE LENGTH of the perianth and the corona is necessary to allocate cultivars to Divisions 1, 2 and 3. A small rule, without any ungraduated portion, is used to measure the length of the outer perianth segment from its junction with the corona (length 'a'). The corona length is measured from the junction with the perianth, with any roll or curl being flattened out (length 'b'). If 'b' is longer than 'a' the cultivar is in Division 1. Where 'b' is less than 'a' but more than one-third of 'a' the cultivar is in Division 2. When 'b' is less than one-third of 'a' the cultivar is in Division 3. Measurements are given at the time of registration and not all cultivars produce the same relative lengths 'a' and 'b' in all growing conditions

Some cultivars may vary in proportion due to different cultural techniques.

Division 3 Small-cupped daffodils. The length of the corona is less than one-third of the length of the perianth.

Division 4 Double daffodils. There is not usually a defined corona and the centre of the flower is a cluster of petaloids. There are no defined criteria of the number of such petaloids but they should be arranged in a pleasing and symmetrical manner. A number of double daffodils have more than one flower per stem, and cultivars such as Cheerfulness are popular as cut blooms. A limited number of double daffodils do retain a complete circular corona, the centre of which is packed with petaloids, eg Petit Four. The petaloids should be of clear colour and evenly arranged within the corona.

Division 5 Triandus daffodils. These include garden hybrids which display the characteristics of *Narcissus triandus*. The main points to look for are:
- usually more than one flower per stem
- delicate necks which allow the heads to droop
- perianth segments sharply reflexed from the corona, narrow and of a silky texture
- corona slightly narrowed at the mouth.

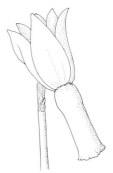

Division 6
cyclamineus hybrid

Division 6 Cyclamineus daffodils. Those garden hybrids which resemble

Narcissus cyclamineus. The major characteristics are:
- usually one flower to a stem
- short neck holding the flower so that the stigma points downwards
- sharply reflexed perianth segments
- narrow cylindrical corona.

jonquilla hybrid, Division 7;

Division 7 Jonquilla daffodils. These have the characteristics of any of the *Narcissus jonquilla* group clearly evident. The various forms of *N jonquilla* are often known as rush-leaved daffodils and they differ in many respects from one another, though all have round stems. The major points to look for in the flowers are:
- more than one flower to a stem, though there are some exceptions
- a characteristic fragrance
- perianth segments held at right angles to the neck, smooth and starlike
- flowers held erect, not pendant.

Division 8 Tazetta daffodils. The tazettas fall into two categories, those with small flowers and those with large flowers, but all are garden hybrids which resemble one of the forms of *Narcissus tazetta.* Characteristics are:
- more than one flower per stem (the small types have four to twenty flowers in one cluster at the end of the stem whilst the large types usually have two, three or four flowers per stem)
- sweet scent
- short bowl-shaped corona
- rounded perianth segments which are held at right angles, or nearly so, to the neck
- perianth segments often crinkled along their length and usually slightly twisted.

tazetta hybrid, Division 8

Division 9 Poeticus daffodils. These must be clearly reminiscent of the forms of *Narcissus poeticus* and be garden hybrids. This often causes some difficulties dependent upon which of the characteristics are perceived as predominant. The main factors are:
- usually one flower per stem
- perianth sparkling white and with clearly visible 'pips' at the tips
- perianth segments usually slightly reflexed from a true right angle
- short flat corona sharply rimmed with red as a minimum of colouring
- distinctive fragrance
- stamens of unequal length so that three anthers, which are globular, are

Poeticus hybrid, Division 9

Even this does not adequately reflect the three main forms:

- corona split for its full length giving six parts that lie flat against each perianth segment giving the impression of a double layer of petals, eg, Chanterelle
- corona split for only part of its length creating ruffled lobes which lie against the perianth, eg, Papillon Blanc
- corona split into distinctly shaped segments, often highlighted by splashes of intense colour, which are flat against the perianth, eg, Lemon Beauty.

held below the three which almost encircle the stigma.

Division 10 Species and wild forms, and wild hybrids. This group embraces many different forms and types in addition to those whose characteristics have been used in the definitions of other Divisions. *Narcissus bulbocodium* species and wild forms are included but induced hybrids, such as Nylon and Muslin, are excluded and classified in Division 12.

Division 11 Split-corona daffodils. A grouping of flowers for which there is no species to be used as a reference. The Division was only created in 1950 and by strict application of the definition many earlier registered cultivars could be equally correctly included. By modern standards the characteristics are:

- usually one flower per stem, though multi-headed types are now being bred
- perianth held at right angles to the neck
- corona split for at least one-third of its length to create six pseudo-petals or frills that lie back against the perianth segments.

In some commercial catalogues the name orchid flowering is being used to describe the split corona cultivars.

split-corona or orchid-flowering cultivar, Division 11

Division 12 Miscellaneous daffodils. This group contains a limited number of induced garden hybrids that cannot with conviction be correctly included in the other Divisions. Often the cultivars arise from the crossing of two dissimilar species so that the progeny do not have a predominance of the characteristics of one species. There are no clear characteristics to qualify a flower for this Division; indeed it is a confusion of characteristics which put a limited number of cultivars in this grouping.

THE STANDARD CULTIVARS

This simple description is often used to denote those cultivars which are likely to be found as relatively tall-growing subjects in the garden. The majority of the generally-accepted standard cultivars are from the trumpets, the large cups, the small cups and the doubles (Divisions 1, 2, 3 and 4 respectively), for example, the widely-known King Alfred (1Y-Y), Fortune (2Y-O), Mrs R. O. Backhouse (2W-P), Ice Follies (2W-W), Golden Harvest (1Y-Y) etc, which are available from garden centres and supermarkets. There are cultivars of similar height from other Divisions which are becoming accepted as standard cultivars and they will certainly enhance most gardens. Splendid, readily-available examples are Suzy (7Y-O), Geranium (8W-O), Liberty Bells (5Y-Y) and Silver Chimes (8W-W).

The standard cultivars have received most of the attention from the hybridisers and are being progressively developed towards the accepted idea of the perfect daffodil. Such breeding programmes have produced a wide range of colours and combinations of colour. Thus, although there are many all-yellow daffodils which satisfy the traditionalists, there are also yellows with red, orange, pink or white coronas as well as similar combinations against a background of white perianths. Recent breeding work has been aimed at producing the all-red daffodil and this looks a distinct possibility as improvements on Altruist (3O-R) and Sabine Hay (3O-R) are being attempted. An all-red trumpet (Division 1) has been imminent for many years;

KING ALFRED (1Y-Y) was registered in 1899 and was then classified as a *Magnicoronati*. A reproduction of an early photograph has been used here to show a true likeness of this cultivar.

17

improved colours are being gradually introduced and some high prices are being paid for orange-coloured cultivars which may be useful in breeding programmes. Perhaps a true red trumpet is to be as elusive as a blue rose.

The standard cultivars are regarded as the true heralds of spring and because of their universal popularity they have been in great demand both as dry bulbs for planting or as cut flowers, though other forms and types may flower earlier. This demand has necessitated the development of systems of propagation that will enable quantities to be achieved much more quickly than would be the case if one were to depend upon natural division of the bulbs. These techniques are still time-consuming but they have made different colour breaks accessible to the majority of gardeners earlier than would be otherwise possible and such beauties as Daydream (2Y-W), a reversed bicolour, Dailmanach (2W-P), a super pink, and Loch Hope (2Y-R), a brightly-coloured masterpiece, will soon be available to grace any garden. The split coronas and other novelties to enchant the flower arrangers, as well as the miniatures, are now widely distributed and satisfy the quest for something more unusual.

Now that so many standard cultivars are becoming available in quantity the old favourites are being joined by quite a retinue such as Saint Keverne (2Y-Y), Spellbinder (1Y-W) and Don Carlos (2W-R), and before too long some of the exhibitors' bankers, such as Kingscourt (1Y-Y), Passionale (2W-P), Empress of Ireland (1W-W) and Rainbow (2W-WWP) will achieve appropriate recognition.

MINIATURES

A miniature is usually regarded as a small-scale version of an original which retains a perfection in its details and has a characteristic grace. Miniature daffodils are cultivars that have naturally small flowers, usually under 2in (5cm) in diameter, held on stems which do not exceed 10in (25cm) in height, except perhaps where they have been forced, but which retain because of their size a unique and characteristic daintiness. Most miniatures are hybrids bred for this daintiness through a combination of a species and a standard cultivar. By definition some of the species are also regarded as true miniature daffodils.

Poor cultivation of standard cultivars can result in flowers which meet either one or both of the size criteria but they lack the essential gracefulness of form. Some of the multi-headed cultivars have individual flowers well under 2in (5cm) in diameter but, again, they are not typically miniatures. Size alone is not a satisfactory criterion for defining a miniature. The exquisite beauty of Segovia (3W-Y), Xit (3W-W), Pequenita (7Y-Y), and the multi-headed cultivars such as Minnow (8W-Y) and Hawera (5Y-Y), is difficult to

MINIATURE DAFFODILS, just like their bigger relations, come in a fantastic range of colours and forms. (Top left) Xit (3W-W); (top centre) Sundial (7Y-Y); (top right) Sun Disc (7Y-Y); (middle left) Bobbysoxer (7Y-YYO); (middle right) Segovia (3W-Y); (lower left) Pencrebar (4Y-Y); (lower right) Minnow (8W-Y). One stem of each is illustrated with a 2p coin for size comparison

surpass and they all have the sparkle and perfection rightly attributed to true miniatures.

In all other respects the miniatures, in spite of their sometimes frail appearance, are just as hardy as the standard cultivars and they require the same level of cultivation and care if they are to produce satisfactory results. Indeed, apart from the characteristics which make them miniatures, they can have the same range of types and forms as the standard cultivars and some of them have their peculiar cultural likes and dislikes.

Miniatures give a good account of themselves in pots as well as the open ground and some of them are ideal subjects for the rockery. Unfortunately, they do not, as yet, have the complete range of colour combinations as found amongst the standard cultivars but there are genuine miniatures from eleven of the twelve recognised Divisions. As they are becoming more popular they may attract more attention from the hybridisers to increase their numbers beyond the hundred or so that are currently available.

SPECIES

There are probably only some sixty or so daffodils that can be regarded as true species. A true species daffodil will breed precisely to type from seed where self-pollination has occurred. Some of those originally thought to be species have now been recognised as natural hybrids, which do not breed true from seed, though some of them are improvements on the species and have been grown on as selected clones.

The species originate in the main from Spain, Portugal and parts of North Africa, and even in this relatively small area there are vast variations of climate and soil. Thus, there needs to be some understanding of these conditions if species are to be successfully grown in the open ground or as 'Alpine' subjects.

Some of the species are reminiscent of the miniatures, and vice versa. They may not have quite the same degree of perfection as assessed for the show-bench but they have a refinement of detail which makes them extremely attractive. *Narcissus watieri* and *N rupicola* are quite charming flowers that have a quality comparable to that of their large show-bench relations, whereas the forms of *N bulbocodium* are often regarded as clowns with their proportionately large coronas and remnants of perianth. Others, such as *N triandus* and *N cyclamineus*, are also individual characters and consequently appealing to many gardeners.

The species produce their flowers at widely differing times, from autumn through to early summer. The autumn-flowering *N viridiflorus* is really the earliest, with its unique all-green flowers, followed by the various forms of *N bulbocodium*, which flower from midwinter through to spring, *N cyclamineus*, flowering in early spring, and the forms of N *jonquilla* and N *tazetta*, flowering through spring and into early summer. So the species not only give some unique characters but also an extended flowering season.

Britain can boast only two native wild daffodils which bear detailed comparison with similar types still occurring naturally in Spain. Indeed, it is suggested that the Tenby daffodil (N *obvallaris*) and the Lent lily (N *pseudo-narcissus*) were brought into Britain by the Romans to provide blooms for decorating their temples and villas. The two wild forms have many similarities and may be closely related as sub-species and to similar daffodils appearing throughout much of central and northern Europe. Whatever their origins, the Tenby daffodil and the Lent lily reigned supreme for many years as heralds of spring and as inspiration to a number of famous writers and poets.

INTERMEDIATE DAFFODILS

This phrase is gradually creeping into the vocabulary of daffodil growers. By definition it is used for those cultivars whose size falls between that of the standard cultivars and that of the miniatures. A simple measurement would be flowers under 3in (7.5cm) in diameter. It is really a categorisation to ensure that the smaller flowers can compete successfully on the show-bench and not be overpowered by their naturally large relations. Indeed, some recent introductions are charming cultivars which may ultimately justify the concept and save themselves from being discarded prematurely.

The concept may be good: it will encourage a concentration on form and colour to prevent some charming flowers being cast into oblivion. However, there is a danger that some standard cultivars will not be grown to their full potential, and exhibited or commercialised as 'intermediate' in an attempt to make them appear useful.

MULTI-HEADED DAFFODILS

Cultivars which produce anything from two to twenty-two, or more, flowers on a single stem are always popular. They hold their condition and colour longer than a single flower, make extremely attractive garden plants and are marvellous for floral art.

Because they are usually closely related to different forms of species daffodil they come in many different styles and colour combinations, as well as different sizes. They often have a strong perfume, which for some people is an additional attraction.

Unfortunately, they have not been given much attention by the hybridisers due to the difficulty of obtaining ripe seed. Thus, some very old cultivars are still popular, for example Grande Monarque (8W-Y), known in the seventeenth century, Silver Chimes (8W-W), registered in 1916, and Trevithian

(7Y-Y) from 1927. More recent cultivars are becoming available and will maintain the tradition, examples being Dickcissel (7Y-W) of 1963, Bell Song (7W-P) of 1971 and Highfield Beauty (8Y-GYO) of 1964. Even newer things from the Rosewarne Experimental Horticultural Stations and from the work of Grant Mitsch in Oregon, USA, promise to ensure a supply of multi-headed cultivars to satisfy most colour and form requirements as well as the consistent demand for cut blooms. The major difficulty is that many cultivars arising from crossing of a hybrid with a species are sterile and cannot therefore be used as the basis of the next, improved, generation.

PERFUMED DAFFODILS

It is not generally appreciated that a number of daffodils produce a characteristic perfume. The majority of those whose scent is most penetrating are near relatives of the various forms of N jonquilla or N tazetta families and the true N poeticus. As with most other perfumed flowers, the sensation is not always popular or pleasant. Although some commercial catalogues now identify the species and cultivars which have a recognisable perfume they do not differentiate between those which are pleasant and those which can be overpowering.

Erlicheer (4W-W) is a very attractive double-flowered cultivar and being of tazetta type is multi-headed; one stem in a warm room very quickly fills every corner with its heady perfume. N jonquilla is not a very tall grower but generates a very pleasant penetrating perfume, especially when in full sun. Geranium (8W-O), Grande Monarque (8W-Y), Sweetness (7Y-Y) and Actea (9W-GYR) are true garden hybrids, all having a bonus of perfume which carries pleasantly across the garden when the blooms are in full sun. N juncifolius, Nylon (12W-W), Pencrebar (4Y-Y) and Hawera (5Y-Y) are true miniatures which are all sweetly scented. N poeticus recurvus, N henriques and N odorus regulosus are species which once established and happy with their environment will be very floriferous and mark their presence with a not unpleasant smell.

In general terms the standard cultivars from Divisions 1, 2, 3 or 4, and the cyclamineus hybrids, do not produce much perfume. A major exception is Fragrant Rose (2W-GPP), registered in 1978 by Brian Duncan, which is not only an outstandingly beautiful pink but highly perfumed. However, the perfume is not typical of daffodils as it is most reminiscent of the rose Super Star (Tropicana in the USA) and is most noticeable when the bulbs are being flowered under glass and the temperature encourages the release of the vapours. It is perhaps a sweeping generalisation, but insufficient attention has been given to the production of perfumed daffodils in spite of the commercial popularity of Cheerfulness and similar cultivars.

22

•2•
Bulbs — Storage and Growth

An understanding of the function and development of the bulbs is as essential as an appreciation of the flowers if good displays are to be achieved year by year. Although a bulb seems to be dormant from summer through to autumn this external appearance is deceptive. Within the bulb there are significant changes taking place as the embryo flower is initiated and formed in all its details. The development of the embryo is critical to the quality of the bloom the following spring. Care and attention given to the bulb during the time it is out of the ground will be repaid with improvements in the performance of the plant in terms of flower production and multiplication of stocks.

TYPES AND SIZES OF BULBS

The quality of the system of cultivation adopted for daffodils has a major influence upon the size of bulbs which are obtained. However, different cultivars produce different types and sizes of bulbs. In general terms, the Division 1 and Division 2 cultivars will produce large solid bulbs which can weigh up to 1lb (450g) whereas the species will produce quite small bulbs, as tiny as peas, with hybrids being of intermediate sizes.

In essence the structure of the bulb is similar to that of an onion. It has a base-plate which is the foundation and which regenerates itself as growth and development take place. The base-plate also develops the root system of the plant from around its circumference; the larger the base-plate the greater the number of roots that are initiated to absorb food, as soluble chemicals, to sustain growth. Damage to the base-plate will limit the number of roots that can be created and once they have been initiated there is only a limited capability to regenerate replacements. A full-size bulb will initiate some thirty to forty roots and can regenerate only three or four of them.

At the centre of the base-plate of each bulb is an apical bud which has the minute structure of the foliage and flower sequence coded within its structure. The evolution of this bud dictates how many leaves are produced each season and whether sufficient leaves are established to release a flowering growth. The central bud is surrounded by scale leaves which are the food storage mechanism of the bulb. Scale leaves are produced annually from the centre

23

Daffodil bulbs develop through a number of stages, splitting to create new independent structures.

A round bulb which is large enough to produce its first flower

A double-nosed bulb showing the first outward signs of division

A triple-nosed bulb with an off-set which could safely be divided from its parent

of the bulb and their number and substance directly affect the size of the bulb. Damage to the scale leaves can cause them to desiccate and be rendered useless for releasing their stored food to the developing leaves and flowers. Surrounding the viable scale leaves are the desiccated remains of scale leaves that have fulfilled their function in earlier seasons — these are usually referred to as the tunic. The colouring of the tunic varies considerably dependent upon the nature of the cultivar and conditions in which it has been grown. There can be up to a dozen layers of the tunic, and splitting and tearing caused by growth of the bulb can create pockets and traps that can play host to scavenging pests. At the top of the bulb remnants of leaves and flower stem will be visible and each grouping represents a 'nose'. It is from each of the noses that new growth will emerge in the following season of growth.

The size of bulb for a particular cultivar is a good guide to the size of bloom that will be obtained, though bulbs produced in different areas will vary. Dutch bulbs are generally larger and looser scaled than say Cornish bulbs but blooms will be comparable.

The sequence of development of bulbs leads to a number of different categories which give variable quality blooms:

Chips Small independent bulbs which will need two or three seasons of growth to reach flowering size and to build up stocks.

Off-sets Independent structures that can be safely separated from the parent bulb with their own piece of base-plate. Large off-sets may be of sufficient size to produce a flower and be the equivalent of a round (see below). Each off-set will have only one nose or point of growth.

Round One complete bulb which is usually circular in cross-section, hence the name, and produces one group of leaves and, when large enough, a flower. The size required to sustain a flower depends very much upon the cultivar. After producing its first flower the interior of the bulb effectively divides to create a large section which may flower and an initiated off-set which will be enclosed by the leaf scales and tunic. Rounds are usually recognised as the bulbs for achieving quality flowers and are preferred by most exhibitors for growing in pots.

A mother bulb which has several off-sets that will need time to reach flowering size

Double-nosed A larger bulb that has two growing points or noses and will produce at least one flower stem from the larger part and possibly a second from the smaller part. Due to the different sizes of the two parts of the bulb there can be significant variations in the size of the flowers. In commercial terms the name is abbreviated as DN and can be quoted as DN1, DN2 or DN3 to give an indication of the size of the bulb. DN1 is the large size which, for the particular cultivar, will be regarded as being of flowering size. Double-nosed bulbs give a good return for border display and for decorative pots where the variation in size is not critical. Their shape allows them to be packed well into troughs and containers to give a wealth of flowers.

Round bulb showing elongated line of the Division 3 and Division 9 cultivars

Triple-nosed A development from a double-nosed bulb. It is usually a double-nosed bulb and large off-set attached to a common base-plate. This type gives a good display in borders. Where possible the off-set should be severed prior to planting and be grown on separately as a way of building up stocks.

A double-nosed bulb showing the dark tunic and spherical shape typical of Division 8

Mother bulb A multi-nosed bulb on one base-plate. It can comprise four or five identifiable small bulbs or as many as twenty small pieces which will ultimately split into independent structures. Mother bulbs give a poor return of flowers and need growing on until all the different pieces can safely be separated and brought back to flowering size. These are usually the biggest bulbs by weight and volume.

A good-sized double-nosed bulb of a miniature; a round, light-skinned bulb of a species, which will divide only very slowly

BUYING BULBS

Once converted to the attractive daffodil cultivars, every grower will seek to enhance the range of colours and types used in the home and garden. However, some cultivars are not likely to be found in the local garden centre and orders will have to be placed with one of the specialist suppliers. Fortunately the range of cultivars available through garden centres is increasing as a positive response to the demands made by customers.

A large proportion of the daffodil bulbs purchased annually is obtained through some form of mail order, and this system can work very well. The principal options are:

Buying by mail order does not give you the opportunity to see the quality of bulbs that you will get for your money. However, most specialist and general suppliers need to retain business and therefore attempt to provide top-quality

Specialist suppliers These have the widest range of cultivars, including many of the more recent introductions. It is usual for the specialists to guarantee that the blooms will be true to name. Prices are often quoted for single units which are supplied as good double-nosed bulbs, though occasionally large rounds will be sent if it is known that the flowers may be used for exhibition work. All bulbs will have been thoroughly cleaned and individually inspected for any visible signs of pests or disease. Most specialists dip the bulbs in their own preferred mix of pesticides and fungicides and thoroughly dry them prior to packing each cultivar in its labelled bag. Bulbs from these suppliers are mailed ready for planting without further treatment.

General suppliers They have a fairly wide range of cultivars but do not include the novelties or very expensive cultivars. Prices fluctuate from supplier to supplier, reflecting the availability of stocks and not necessarily the quality of the bulbs. Except for the species, the bulbs will be good quality double-nose (DN1, though occasionally DN2) but may not have had old roots or loose tunic removed. Bulbs from these general suppliers will be received in the autumn and should be unpacked upon receipt and cleaned of old roots and tunic so that signs of pests and disease can be located and any valid complaints lodged. The major attention should be given to checking for any apparent softness of the bulbs. Often the cultivars are guaranteed true to name but some inadvertent mixing of cultivars does arise.

Special offers Usually a number of retailers advertise special offers of daffodil bulbs in a restricted range of cultivars. Such offers may appear attractive but the quality and size of bulbs can be extremely variable and can bring a range of problems into an otherwise healthy garden. Poor-sized bulbs take just as much effort to get planted and the yield of flowers in the following season can be disappointing. As with most garden plants, purchases from reputable sources may be a little more expensive but the initial returns of blooms will be worth the additional expenditure.

bulbs that have been properly grown, stored and treated for pests. If for any reason the bulbs received are not satisfactory most suppliers will deal promptly with justifiable and itemised complaints.

Bulbs available through garden centres come in a much narrower range of cultivars but fortunately this is extending year by year. As the majority of garden centres buy in bulbs for resale the main concern is a rapid turnover and in some cases the environments in which they are stored and displayed are far from ideal. It is essential to pay regular visits during late summer so that as soon as the daffodil bulbs become available they can be purchased and stored in conditions which are as near correct as you can make them. Pre-packed bulbs are increasingly popular with the staff of garden centres as they are convenient to display and handle. From a buyer's point of view they severely limit the ability to check the quality of the bulbs and especially restrict the testing for signs of softness. Bulbs in boxes may encourage impulse purchases but, if there is a choice, leave them and go for the bulbs which can be handled and selected for evenness of size and type to give a more even display. If the bulbs are in net containers try to feel each one for any telltale signs of softness and select the pack which has bulbs of a uniform size and type. Where bulbs are displayed in the traditional partitioned boxes there is always a risk that some mixing of cultivars may have taken place. These display boxes now contain a wider choice of cultivars, especially of the miniatures and species. Before selecting your bulbs be sure you know what you are going to use them for and aim to have a balance between sheer size and number of noses. Mother bulbs will look the largest, especially where the bulbs have not been cleaned of roots and tunic, but they will give a display of variable quality.

General retailers and supermarkets are tending to carry stocks of the more common cultivars and rely upon impulse purchasing. The bulbs are well packaged and displayed so that they cannot be checked before purchase. Most are of reasonably good quality but the packaging and the environment in the storerooms and selling areas is not usually suitable. If purchases are made from these outlets the bulbs should be taken from the boxes as soon as possible and stored in cool airy conditions until you are ready to plant them.

Amateur breeders and exhibitors will extend their searches for newer cultivars to the other side of the world. Air mail facilities are now able to keep the time spent in transit to a reasonable minimum but are expensive and can only be justified for the recently-introduced novelties. Where bulbs are crossing international barriers the Plant Health Authorities in the receiving country will require detailed certificates of plant health which have been checked by their equivalent bodies two or three times during the preceding season of growth. The costs incurred in obtaining certification and the additional paperwork are an extra burden that has to be borne by the purchaser. Direct imports can be very expensive but often it is the only way to ensure early availability of the newer cultivars or those that have established favourable reputations in their country of origin as numbered seedlings.

Bulbs ordered from another country in the same hemisphere, say USA to England, will have experienced broadly the same pattern of seasons. There may be some slight difference in terms of the months but they will be received in the autumn as a natural period. The few extra days spent in air mail transit should not have done too much harm. As soon as they are received the package should be opened and each bulb be given free access to cool air. The aim should be to plant the bulbs as soon as possible after receipt and ideally within twenty-four hours of the package being opened. Such bulbs should produce their flowers the following spring at approximately their normal flowering date.

Where bulbs are being imported from the opposite hemisphere, for example New Zealand to England, the difference in seasons creates an additional complication. In deepest winter, catalogues will have to be obtained and orders placed as soon as possible. Air mail is a must as any other method of transport will cause severe deterioration of the bulbs. Special plans need to be made so that pots and compost are available and accessible for use when the bulbs are received in early spring. The bulbs should be planted as soon as they are received and they will be expecting autumn conditions and a winter of root and embryo development. The containers should be kept cool, without actually becoming frozen, for as long as possible to maximise the chances of good root systems developing. Even so, the bulbs can be expected to produce flowers in late summer and then undergo a fairly rapid die-back. If given sensible post-flowering attention they will survive, though they will probably lose some weight and substance. The second year's growth will conform to the prevailing seasons and in about three years the bulbs will have fully adjusted to the different timing of the seasons. Thus, importing in this way is a long-term project and the true potential of the cultivars should be assessed only after they have stabilised in the different environment.

STORAGE OF BULBS

Once bulbs are lifted at the end of the growing season (see page 00) they are effectively exposed to a potentially alien environment. It is important that the best possible conditions are maintained to avoid deterioration of the bulb and to reduce the risk of damage to the embryo flower as it begins its development. The different cultivars respond in different ways to external stimuli and some, such as Division 9 (poeticus hybrids), will naturally commence initiation of roots within a week or two of the old ones fading. Storage conditions should try to create an environment which does not encourage external signs of growth. The shorter the period of time that daffodil bulbs are out of the ground the better. Ideally the bulbs should be replanted within six weeks of being lifted but they can, with care, be kept viable for up to five months.

As the bulbs are lifted (see page 52 for method) they should be placed in bags made of plastic netting. These can be specially made from lengths of Netlon tubing, available from garden centres, or they can be recycled bags which have been used as packaging of produce, particularly vegetables, at supermarkets. Each cultivar should be placed in a separate bag and have an identification label attached with wire or twine. The newly-lifted bulbs will have some soil or compost adhering to their tunics and this will hold mois-ture, so they must be dried before being placed in storage. The temptation is to leave them on the ground exposed to the sun to give fairly rapid drying but this can cause the temperature of the bulbs to rise with consequential risk of damage to the tiny internal buds. It is preferable to dry bulbs in a cool sheltered spot, away from direct sunlight, using an electric fan to blow air across and through them to hasten the process.

There is an inevitable risk that diseases may develop and spread through bulbs whilst they are in storage. To counteract this possibility most specialist growers dip their bulbs in a fungicide solution within twenty-four hours of them being lifted. This is usually done by first of all washing the bags of bulbs in water, which is at the ambient temperature, to remove some of the adhering soil which can reduce the life and effectiveness of the chemical dip.

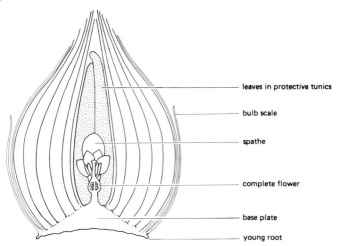

leaves in protective tunics

bulb scale

spathe

complete flower

base plate

young root

THE BULB YOU BUY may give the impression of being dormant but internally it is developing the embryo plant as an identifiable unit. By early autumn there is a tiny plant, perfect in every detail, gradually enlarging to be ready for the external stages of growth. Embryo roots are ready to emerge from the base-plate and forage for water and nutrients. The tiny flower, correct in all of its details is enclosed in the spathe. The young leaves will remain yellow in their protec-tive tunic until light stimulates the release of chlorophyll. The majority of the bulb is filled by the fleshy scale leaves that provide the initial food for the development of the leaves and flower

The bulbs are allowed to drain and are then immersed in a fungicide solution for twenty minutes. Suitable preparations are 0.5 per cent formaldehyde, or a benomyl solution made up to the manufacturer's recommended strength, or combinations of chemicals (see Chapter 7). After immersion the bulbs must be fully dried, and checked carefully to ensure that water is not being retained between the necks, especially of the double-nosed and mother forms.

Storing the dried bulbs in trays is the most convenient way of using the available space. These trays must be capable of being stacked, and have wire netting or slotted bases to permit free circulation of air around and amongst the bulbs. Sufficient trays are necessary to ensure that the bulbs are not tightly packed in many layers as this will restrict movement of air. Alternatively, the netting bags of bulbs can be suspended from a clothes-horse, which will allow good air circulation, or from a framework or the rafters of the storage space. However, as hot air rises the temperatures at roof or ceiling level will be higher than at ground level and hanging near the roof will expose the bulbs to greater risk.

All trays or boxes should be thoroughly cleaned before being pressed into service. Containers which were used the previous year for storage of daffodils may still harbour debris from the bulbs or traces of diseased material which can be reactivated by poor storage conditions. The old standby, Jeyes Fluid, is a useful solution for scrubbing the trays clean and reducing the risks of spreading infection.

Temperature during storage is critical. Ideally, a fairly constant temperature not exceeding 60°F (15.5°C) should be maintained for the full period of storage. A cool, well-ventilated cellar is preferable but with modern building systems this is rarely available unless one can be borrowed at one's workplace or at a friend's house. Most people have to make do with a garage, shed or outhouse, and in this eventuality steps should be taken to ensure that the ventilation is good and that there is enough draught to keep the air circulating and give some control over the excesses of temperature. The nature of the structure and its location can significantly affect the range of temperatures created; for example, a wooden garden shed which is in full sunlight can, during the height of summer, have daily internal temperatures varying from 50°F (10°C) to 105°F (40°C). It is good practice to keep a reliable maximum/minimum thermometer amongst the bulbs in store and to look for alternative facilities if the temperatures are liable to wide fluctuation. Where temperatures go above 70°F (21°C) and there is any dampness in the atmosphere the conditions are likely to encourage the development and rapid spread of disease.

As soon as convenient the stored bulbs should be cleaned. Each bulb, with its associated off-sets, should be carefully rubbed clean of any adhering soil and the withered roots should be gently pulled off to expose the base-plate.

GOOD STORAGE CONDITIONS should be provided for the bulbs once they have been dried off. In plastic mesh netting bags, they can hang from a clothes-horse and rails until totally dry. Once dry they can be cleaned and sorted ready for replanting. An electric fan gives forced air circulation which helps to keep the bulbs cool

Removal of the roots requires great care, with small sections being pulled away in a circular motion. The remnants of the foliage should also be removed. The objective should be to have a shiny-surfaced bulb that can be examined carefully for any signs of pests or disease. Care should be taken when removing any of the outer scales from the bulb that the white-fleshed scales are not exposed as this will encourage deterioration. The scales and roots may not be sufficiently dry the first time the bulbs are checked and if it appears that damage is being caused, do as much as possible but leave the final cleaning until the next checking.

Particular attention should be directed towards the base-plate for signs of any incursion into the bulb by the grub of the narcissus fly or for any areas which have gone soft and dark brown (a sure sign of basal rot). Rotting of the base-plate accompanied by a white woolly deposit is a clear indication of an infection by eelworm. The neck of the bulb should also be examined for any

31

signs of softness or discoloration, which would be indicative of fungal prob-lems or perhaps a sign that the central scales of the bulb have been eaten away by a grub of a narcissus fly. A gentle squeeze of the bulb will also be helpful as a further check for deterioration — a healthy bulb should feel very solid and not compress under reasonable finger and thumb pressure. Although one should be vigilant in checking the bulbs one must not become obsessed with the prospects of finding signs of disease or pests — they do arise but with sensible cultivation they should be rarely seen. This cleaning and checking process may be repeated to good advantage two or three times during the short period that the bulbs are out of the ground. Chapter 7 gives details of the pests and diseases most likely to affect daffodils and describes methods of dealing with them.

It is essential to have some system which can identify the origins of bulbs which are being kept in storage. This is particularly relevant where pot culture has been used for either home decoration or the production of exhibition blooms (see Chapters 4 and 5) and those bulbs should not be used for the same purpose in the following season. A simple but effective system is to use different coloured netting bags for bulbs that have come from different loca-tions. Alternatively, different coloured plastic wire can be used to fasten the labels to each bag. Such colour coding systems can become very sophisticated but clearly assist in readily identifying the origins of the bulbs and help to ensure that the best bulbs possible are allocated to the different uses at planting time. It is important also that the size of the mesh of the netting is appropriate to the size of the bulbs. A very fine mesh needs to be used for bulbs of species and miniatures if they are not to be forced through the netting and separated from their correct label. Mixing of stocks of different cultivars will necessitate at least a year of growth before the bulbs can be identified and returned to the correct batch.

PREPARING FOR REPLANTING

As the bulbs are cleaned and handled during storage, assessments can be made of their quality and suitability for different uses. The exhibitor will keep records of those cultivars which have good rounds or large double-nosed bulbs so that checks can be made that a good range is available to match the schedule definitions of potential classes. Where a container display is required for home decoration those cultivars with a large number of even-sized double-nosed bulbs will be similarly identified. Acknowledging that replanting should take place as early as reasonably practicable, a sequence will have to be established. The general order of priority, subject to availability of bulbs, especially new stocks being obtained, would be to plant:

- Pots and bowls: where these are going to be forced into flower much earlier than their natural dates.
- Species and miniatures: to get them back to a natural environment and reduce the risk of bulb deterioration.
- Pots for exhibition: to give as long a period of growth, in particular root development, before they are brought into their protected environment.
- Open ground: laying out border arrangements as soon as any spaces can be cleared, and filling the prepared exhibition beds as early as possible.
- Troughs, window boxes etc: as soon as summer displays have finished.

The aim is to have everything completed by late autumn. The only exceptions to this sequence would be the early-flowering species and specially-prepared bulbs, such as Paperwhite Grandiflora, which do not have the same requirements for periods exposed to cool conditions.

The principles of garden cultivation are fully explained in Chapter 3, and Chapter 4 describes a variety of techniques for special plantings and indoor displays. However, a certain amount of preparation while the bulbs are still in storage will help planting to proceed smoothly. The required pots, containers, labels, composts, fertilisers etc can be gathered together in advance. All pots and containers should be identified against lists of the bulbs available for different uses and must be thoroughly cleaned; ideally they should be soaked and scrubbed in a sterilising solution, such as Jeyes Fluid, and stacked under cover. Attention must also be given to preparing ground that is to receive bulbs. Well-worked soil will make the task of planting that much easier and interruptions to remove stones, incursive roots etc will be avoided.

The final stage of the storage period is often most important as the bulbs will not be seen again for at least nine months, and possibly a lot longer. After a final visual check the bulbs should have another fungicide dip to prevent the spread of basal rot and this may be accompanied by treatment against the ravages of the narcissus fly. Most keen exhibitors will use proprietary chemicals in either powder or liquid form to protect against 'fly'. Use of chemical treatments and dips needs to be kept in a sensible proportion.

During the storage period it is also possible to carry out the 'hot water' treatment of the bulbs. This is aimed at killing bulb scale mites and similar debilitating organisms, in particular the narcissus eelworm which can result in the rapid decimation of stocks. The procedure is quite simply to immerse the bulbs in water which is kept at a constant temperature of 112°F (44.4°C) for one hour, but the equipment to achieve this is not readily available and unless the bulbs are extremely valuable or required for a breeding programme it may be better to discard them if they are suspected of harbouring mites.

Some amateurs have developed their own equipment but even so they probably find that some of the flowers in the following season are badly distorted because the treatment was carried out at the wrong time in relation to the development of the embryo and they could not afford to cut open a bulb of each cultivar to check that the embryo was at the appropriate stage. General growth following hot water treatment may appear weakened and distorted but one year later the full benefits will be seen with solid healthy foliage building up a very substantial bulb. Various chemical substances have proved reasonably successful as alternatives to hot water treatment but these are expensive, require special equipment and can have residual effects. Some such treatments are used by large commercial growers but they should be considered by amateurs only where the value of the affected bulbs is very high or they are needed for a future breeding programme. Few chemical treatments are 100 per cent successful and some resistance to their effects can be built up by the eelworm and scale mites.

Once they have been cleaned, sorted and dipped the bulbs are ready for replanting. All that remains is to sever the large off-sets so that they can be given sufficient space in which to develop. The off-set needs to be well clear of the tunic of the main bulb and should be cut off with a very sharp knife or scalpel which has been sterilised immediately prior to each cut so that undetected health problems are not transferred to the next bulb. It would also be prudent to ensure that any cut surface is dusted with flowers of sulphur to discourage infection getting into the bulb.

For mass planting it is advisable to have a good mix of bulbs of different sizes for each cultivar which can be well spaced out so that the small off-sets have room to develop and can produce blooms in succeeding years. By planting only double-nosed bulbs a good display will be achieved in the first year but in succeeding years it may take time for them to produce a comparable display. During the final stages of storage those cultivars which are to be

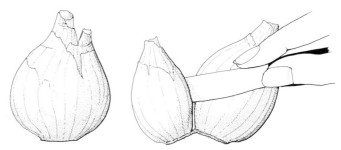

DURING STORAGE, bulbs should be cleaned and graded ready for replanting. On the left is a tight double-nosed bulb (DN1) which is ideal for packing into pots to give a good display of colour. The bulb on the right has developed a large off-set which is still attached to its parent at the base-plate. Prior to replanting, the off-set should be severed from its parent with a clean, sharp knife so that it can be planted with sufficient room in which to develop

planted in the mixed border can be spaced along suitable lengths of Netlon tubing so as to be ready for planting. This is a time-consuming job but well worth the effort if clumps of daffodils are going to be close together, so that at lifting time they can be kept as separate cultivars. The Netlon tubing needs to have a fairly large mesh to ensure that the shoots can pass through without damage.

PROPAGATION OF STOCKS

Whilst bulbs are in store some attempts can be made to encourage rapid multiplication of numbers. Natural multiplication only slowly creates new bulbs and it is worth experimenting with techniques that can give an increased return, especially on choice cultivars which are difficult to obtain from commercial sources.

Propagation of garden hybrids depends upon the ability to encourage the bulb to divide and produce off-sets which can be separated from the parent. The speed with which this process can be achieved depends upon the cultivar and upon the quality of the cultivation technique being adopted. By annual lifting of bulbs and the severing of off-sets which are attached only at the base-plate it is possible to increase the rate of division but, even so, a considerable time is needed to create commercial stocks of a particular cultivar. The species, being capable of re-creating themselves by seed, generally have a much slower rate of bulb division and do not respond well to attempts to hasten the process. However, seed can be obtained by self-pollination, enabling stocks of species to be built up.

Various experimental projects have been attempted to find ways of encouraging a much more rapid system of initiating new bulbs. It has been observed that bulbs ravaged by the narcissus fly have some ability to initiate new growth from the undamaged part of the base-plate even though the centre of the bulb has suffered major damage. This has led to a variety of techniques for cutting the bulb into segments of various sizes and keeping these in controlled conditions such that small bulbs are initiated. The small bulbs take four or five years to reach flowering size and, indeed, may take even longer to get to the point of matching the original bulb in terms of quality of flower and consistency of performance. As practised by commercial growers the technique is known as 'twin-scaling' and there are derivatives such as 'quartering' and 'chipping' which do not give the same potential yield of bulblets. This process is enabling vast quantities to be produced and selected cultivars to be available from general outlets at realistic prices. Each year many tons of bulbs (each representing about 20,000 bulbs) are twin-scaled or chipped to attempt to satisfy demand, especially for expendable bulbs that can be used for forcing.

35

Essentially the technique for twin-scaling is simple and can be used by the amateur. It falls into a number of stages:

Stage 1 A round bulb is carefully cleaned of all roots and loose brown tunic and has its nose cut off parallel to the base. It is then sterilised in a solution of 1 per cent formaldehyde for five minutes.

Stage 2 A sharp knife is used to cut longitudinal segments about ⅜in (10mm) thick at the outer surface of the bulb.

Stage 3 Each segment is laid on its side and by careful cutting through the base-plate, pairs of fleshy leaf-scales are created, each pair having its own portion of base-plate attached. The outer papery tunic and the small inner scales are discarded.

Stage 4 The twin-scales are disinfected in 0.2 per cent benomyl solution for thirty minutes and transferred into thin-gauge plastic bags containing damp vermiculite (or other sterile water-retaining material).

Stage 5 The bags are sealed, leaving an airspace above the vermiculite, and set aside for incubation. A temperature of 68°F (20°C) should be maintained for the incubation period of twelve weeks. Small bulbils should develop between the pairs of scales on the remnant of base-plate. Realistically some twenty-five to thirty-five bulbils can be expected from each original bulb, even allowing for some losses.

Stage 6 The bulbils are planted out 1½ to 2in (4 to 5cm) deep in frost-free conditions, and lifted and replanted as they fill the allotted space.

The equipment needed for this technique is readily available in most homes. A sharp carving or kitchen knife can be used for cutting the bulbs, and can be sterilised with methylated spirits between each one. Unused polythene storage bags are effectively sterilised on their inner surface and by cutting a bag open a suitable working surface can be created. The storage of the twin-scales in one of these bags is ideal. The major difficulty is finding storage space, for the incubation process, which can be maintained at the required temperature.

It is suggested by some researchers that as soon as bulbs 4in (10cm) in circumference are achieved the process can be repeated. Good cultivation should give bulbs of sufficient size after three years. In this way even more rapid rates of multiplication can readily be achieved.

Twin-scaling enables the rapid multiplication of stocks of a given cultivar, for example:

	Number of bulbs produced				
	Start	4 years	8 years	16 years	24 years
Realistic natural division — double every other year	1 bulb	4	16	256	4,000
Twin-scaling	1 bulb	30	900	810,000	729,000,000

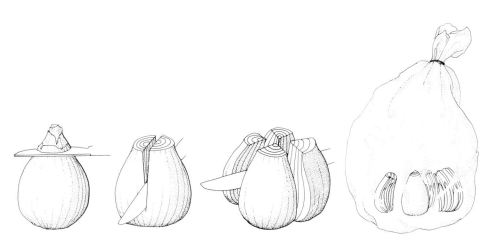

CHIPPING OF BULBS is a relatively simple technique available to amateur growers for increasing the rate of multiplication of a favourite cultivar. The main stages are: (1) the neck section is cut from a cleaned round bulb; (2) the bulb is cut in half with a clean, sharp knife; (3) further cuts are made to create four or more pieces, each having a portion of the base-plate; (4) the pieces are incubated in a sealed plastic bag to encourage development of bulbils between the scale leaves. Bulbils will need to be grown for three to four years to reach flowering size and each new plant will be identical to the original cultivar

Chipping, as a technique, is similar to twin-scaling and was originally used by the Glasshouse Crops Research Institute (GCRI) for the rapid multiplication of virus-free Grand Soleil d'Or for the Isles of Scilly. The operation is as described for twin-scaling except that stages 2 and 3 are replaced by a single operation of cutting the bulb longitudinally into $1/2$, $1/4$, $1/8$ or $1/16$ portions. On a commercial scale some success is achieved with bulk incubation in trays using a grit/peat medium. Fewer bulbils are produced but the easier technique and greater speed make it a viable system that can be practised without the resources of a laboratory. On an amateur scale, chipping to produce $1/4$ sections of the original bulb gives a very realistic return and is well worth attempting.

Even more rapid propagation is possible using the technique known as tissue culture. Although many experiments are being carried out, the technique is usually most successful where adequate laboratory facilities are available. However, tissue culture is of tremendous value as it enables virus-free stocks to be re-established that can then be increased by twin-scaling or chipping. In essence, the technique depends upon the ability of a small piece of plant tissue (referred to as an explant) when exposed to rich nutrient (in a jelly-like medium) to postpone normal growth and create cell clusters that can be further divided into 'fragments'. These fragments can again be exposed to rich nutrients to multiply or they can be encouraged to develop into normal plants by a change of chemicals in the jelly-like medium. Throughout the procedures sterile conditions are important and temperature and light are critical to success. These conditions are not readily available to most amateurs and tissue culture is more suited to commercial operations.

•3•
Principles of Garden Cultivation

Daffodils are wonderfully tolerant garden plants and have a degree of hardiness which enables them to give splendid displays year in and year out. Because of their ability to thrive in most settings it is too often assumed that they will grow well without human intervention or assistance.

The vast majority of daffodils poke their shoots and then their flowers into the forefont of any garden display at the time of year when most subjects are still struggling to recover from the traumas of winter. This makes the whole genus especially welcome as a colourful start to the gardening year. However, during this time they are coping with extremes of temperature, hail, sleet and snow, and their resilience to these conditions, and ability to stand up straight after a covering of snow, gives much pleasure. Naturally the foliage and stems are fading away as most other garden subjects are bursting into active growth and there is a danger that we assume that we can tidy them up and rely upon them doing as well next year.

Giving attention to the requirements of the plant is not difficult. The adoption of a few basic principles will ensure that this year's wonderful display will be repeated next year and in subsequent years. So we will see the results of our efforts in the array of blooms. Daffodils are individuals but as a genus they are relatively trouble free. There are a few pests and diseases (see Chapter 7) but good cultivation will ensure that the miracle of bulb production, by division, yields a rich harvest of clean, healthy and solid material that is more likely to be resistant to the problems causing weak or poor growth.

As we are dealing with general principles it has been assumed that all cultivars and species will respond in the same way. Fortunately, the vast majority will enjoy the attention though one or two may not and appropriate notes of exceptions are made. Specialist conditions and treatments are identified in Chapter 4.

The overriding principle must be the encouragement of a full cycle of growth in the most favourable conditions possible. This means the provision of food, light and water in ways and at times that match the varying requirements which arise in the annual cycle of growth. Some requirements can be provided quite simply whereas others may not be feasible in a given environment and compensations should be made.

SOID

Garden hybrid daffodils are not too particular about the soil in which they are grown and any well-cultivated ground will be adequate. However, if something better than adequate is required, attention needs to be given to the mechanical working of the soil to ensure that the roots have a good and free run to a relatively large depth.

Alkalinity/acidity (as measured by pH) is often critical for plants if they are to have access to essential elements, usually potassium, nitrogen and phosphorus, and the trace elements vital for proper metabolism. The pH affects the ability of the elements to be released from the chemical compounds contained in fertilisers. Experimental work on the effects of various soil pH conditions as applicable to daffodils is relatively limited. However, it is well known that leading exhibitors are able to produce excellent blooms and achieve good bulb increase with a fairly broad banding around the neutral condition (pH7). A slightly acid condition (around pH6.5) will suit most cultivars and species, though only rarely does any special attention need to be given to significant alteration of the pH. The liming of soils for daffodils is not necessary unless the soil is very acid, and treatments appropriate to previous crops should be sufficient. Applications of calcified seaweed do have some benefit to the intensity of colour but this comes from the trace elements and the calcium content does not appear to influence yield of bulbs or flowers.

Roots of daffodils must be able to breathe and any compacted soil will be injurious to the plant. Soil which has been worked for a previous crop or prior to planting will contain about 40 per cent of its volume in the form of voids which can be occupied by water or air. The presence of small stones or grits will ensure that there are voids which will drain free of water and draw air into the soil to the benefit of the growth of the plant. Grits and stones will also help to prevent too much compaction of the ground, especially where there is a risk of pressure, for instance when a planted area in grass has to be cut. Stones larger than walnut size do not readily reduce compaction and can impede the development of roots and the emerging shoot, and lateral development of the bulb and off-sets: their removal may be a tedious exercise but it is of great benefit.

Any soil which has been worked for a previous crop will contain a reasonable amount of humus which will help retain moisture that can be absorbed by the roots. A high humus content implies high water retention, which is not appreciated by most daffodils. Some species, such as *Narcissus cyclamineus*, are tolerant of high humus content whereas others, such as *N tazetta* and its hybrids, are more tolerant of low humus which enables the soil to dry out quicker in the summer period. The addition of humus, be it peat or rotted compost, should be avoided unless the soil has become very impoverished, as may be the case in an established shrub border, or it is very sandy in composition.

Most daffodils require an adequate supply of water but they cannot tolerate stagnant water and great care should be taken to ensure that localised water pockets are not created by deep cultivation at a specific point in the border, grass or garden. Where the ground has a natural slope it is unlikely that such traps will exist though underlying clay or rocks may create difficulties.

PLANTING OF BULBS

Care at the time of planting will significantly influence development in the first season and lay a proper foundation for future years. Careless planting may leave voids under or around the bulbs which can hold water and encourage spread of disease.

Depth of planting is important. Too great a depth will deplete the bulb as it forces the shoot to the surface and the conditions which will permit photosynthesis to take place. Too shallow a planting may expose the bulb to extremes of temperature and encourage excessive splitting into off-sets, which may be good for bulb increase but disastrous for blooms in subsequent years. A general rule of thumb is to have soil above the neck of the bulb to a depth equivalent to twice the height of the bulb. It is always preferable to plant too deep rather than too shallow. Where daffodils are to be overplanted with, say, summer bedding or annuals, a greater depth of planting will enable the ground to be hoed or weeded without risk of damage to the bulbs. The extra depth will mean that the flowers will come a few days later than would otherwise be the case from that cultivar. Daffodils, having roots which run deep, can usually compete with shallow-rooted annuals, grass etc, but do not welcome close association with deep-rooted weeds or perennials.

The distance between the bulbs is also critical. Each bulb needs sufficient space to allow for lateral movement of developing off-sets. The desired effect of the display must be taken into account but for good growth the ideal is to allow twice the diameter of the bulb as the distance from its neighbour. Closer planting will give a closer mass of flowers but reduce the yield of bulbs.

N. CYCLAMINEUS ALWAYS MAKES AN IMPRESSIVE SIGHT when planted in clumps. Early line drawings of this species were considered to be too improbable and eccentric but then the actual flowers were rediscovered in Spain by Peter Barr (1890). The reflexing style of perianth is a major characteristic of Division 6 cultivars, the cyclamineus hybrids

TRIPARTITE (11Y-Y) one of the few multi-headed examples of split corona daffodils and an interesting form from this very variable Division

BOLD PLANTINGS OF DAFFODILS
in shaped beds give a wonderul
display of colour to brighten the
early spring
ACROPOLIS (4W-R) is a popular
tall growing double daffodil that
makes an outstanding display in
the garden

KINGSCOURT (1Y-Y) holder of
First Class Certificates for various
uses and to many people a typical
form of daffodil

The tolerance of the daffodil is clearly evidenced in its ability to grow and flower even if it is not planted at the correct time of the year. The timing of planting will be influenced by the availability of bulbs from suppliers, immediate availability of space in the garden and, to a lesser extent, by climatic considerations or the facilities for storing bulbs. The earlier the bulbs can be planted the better they will respond and in some senses the conditions in the ground are more favourable to the health of the bulbs than inadequate storage conditions. Ideally, daffodils should be planted in early autumn if they are available. Later planting may give satisfactory crops of blooms the following spring but the effect on the root system may limit the development of the bulbs for future years — the longer the delay the greater the potential effect on a bulb's ability to sustain itself. Autumn and winter-flowering species and cultivars should be replanted as soon as possible after lifting and sorting.

PLANTING IN A BORDER is best done by taking out a large hole, 8in (20cm) deep, well clear of foliage or shrubs. The base of the hole should be well worked and have fertiliser incorporated. The bulbs stand on a layer of gravel and are spaced along a plastic netting tube to facilitate subsequent lifting and isolation of different cultivars planted close together

A GRACEFUL and colourful plastic tub which can be moved to brighten a dull corner in early spring. The daffodils are Dove Wings (6W-Y) which do not grow very tall and eliminate the need for staking. The edging is *Scilla tubergeniana*

Individual preference will dictate the method of planting, be it in a prepared trench or area, or separate holes to accommodate each bulb. Whichever approach is adopted some advantage may be gained by having a shallow layer of 1/4in (3 to 5mm) washed gravel as the surface in which the base of the bulb is embedded. As the bulbs are covered with soil to the required depth, care should be taken to keep them in an upright position to encourage even development of off-sets. A bulb planted on its side will grow and produce a flower but the extra distance through which the shoot travels will cause unnecessary depletion of the bulb and it will need greater regeneration time.

Where different cultivars are planted in close proximity without precautions being taken to segregate them, problems may be encountered if and when the bulbs are lifted again. Plastic materials which do not rot or disintegrate when buried in soils are of practical importance here. Expandable net tubing (Netlon) is very useful as bulbs can be spaced along its length and at the time of planting they can be distributed in a way which gives a balanced effect. The size of the mesh must be large enough to allow foliage to pass through without restriction or damage, but small enough to retain off-sets that will be produced. The use of net tubing has been extensively practised in research establishments, where it is essential to ensure that all bulbs are recovered at lifting time, and appears to have no harmful effects. Rigid plastic containers can also be used provided that they do not have solid sides or bases which would restrict the ability of the roots to forage for water and food. Indeed plastic baskets filled with planted bulbs can be buried at strategic points in the border and after the flowers have finished their display can be lifted and moved to a sheltered spot to allow the growth cycle to be completed. In this way the bulbs and roots are not damaged and the area is available earlier than normal for the planting of a summer display.

FERTILISERS

The facility with which naturalised bulbs produce their blooms has given rise to the misconception that daffodils can survive with an absolute minimum of nourishment, but correctly balanced feeding will pay dividends over the years. Certain types of fertiliser should be avoided if soft bulbs, susceptible to disease, are not to be produced. Others are traditionally advocated but they are being superseded by modern complex inorganic chemicals which can be tailored to be totally compatible with the needs of the bulb at different stages of development.

It has been well established that any fertiliser is a mixture of chemicals able to release the elements nitrogen (N), phosphorus (P) and potassium (K) into the soil and in a form (usually soluble ions) that can be absorbed by the roots. Nitrogen encourages lush foliage and this ensures that a large volume of leaf material is available to generate food for replenishing the bulb. However, too much nitrogen can create a softer bulb more susceptible to disease and so it needs to be used sparingly. Phosphorus encourages the formation of strong effective roots and gives strength to the whole plant. However, it is potassium that is essential for the production of solid and ripened bulbs ready for next year's display. In addition to the basic elements, the chosen fertiliser should contain a proportion of the trace elements, such as magnesium, boron, iron etc, as these will ensure that the plant is able to realise its true potential, especially in the colouring of the bloom.

Organic materials from plant and animal wastes can be used, but very sparingly unless they are well rotted. In this well-decayed state their efficiency as a source of the essential elements is questionable but they do have great benefit through increasing the humus content of the soil. Fresh organic materials are usually high in nitrogen which does encourage good foliage but does not help the bulb to build a solid structure for subsequent years. Materials applied in the previous season for other crops will usually have been well rotted and incorporated into the soil and will therefore be extremely useful.

Other organic materials, such as bone meal or hoof and horn, are favoured as a source of phosphates held in a state which permits slow release into the soil. They also contain a small proportion of nitrogen which is not excessive at any phase of the growth cycle. They are most suitable for application at planting time and under the bulbs where the conditions favour slower release into the area of root activity.

Fresh wood ash from the bonfire contains a quantity of potassium salts and these can be a useful supplement to meet the needs of the bulbs in spring. As the potassium salts are readily soluble, wood ash should be stored in dry conditions as soon as it can be handled. The application of wood ash can be made in early spring and in addition to providing some nutrients can improve the soil condition.

The significant developments of inorganic compounds and mixtures of different complex salts have been largely geared to production of food crops but they can be of great benefit to daffodils. Autumn dressing with a low-nitrogen compound of slow-release formulation will take care of the majority of the bulbs' nutritional requirements. This can be supplemented in spring by a liquid fertiliser which is balanced or veering to high potash and after the flowers have faded any high-potash liquid fertiliser (or readily soluble salt such as K_2SO_4 — sulphate of potash) will ensure that the plant has the soluble ion which is so essential to the formation of healthy solid bulbs. Specially formulated liquid fertilisers designed for tomatoes have an N:P:K availability that is compatible with the needs of daffodils from the time the foliage emerges through to die-back and the proportion of potassium will help with the production of good bulbs.

Foliar feeding can play a useful part in a programme of providing essential nutrients at the time they are needed or to stimulate growth. Again, proprietary products can be utilised if their analysis is appropriate, even though they may have been designed for other subjects. With daffodils it is necessary to add a wetting agent to the solution to improve adhesion of the droplets to the foliage so that they can be absorbed. Special wetters are used in commercial plantings but liquid detergents serve the same purpose.

WATERING

In the normal patterns of the seasons the water requirements of the daffodil are satisfied. There are two periods in the cycle where additional water can aid the plant to maximise its growth thereby enhancing the effectiveness of future displays.

Early initiation of roots in the late summer/early autumn period is essential if they are to develop and extend well away from the immediate neighbour-hood of the bulb to where nutrient availability should be greater. Water acts as a stimulus to root initiation and if the soil remains dry due to lack of rain or competition from other large plants the trigger mechanisms will not function. For choice bulbs, watering to compensate for lack of rain will be beneficial.

Towards the other end of the growth cycle, additional water, with or without the incorporation of liquid fertilisers, will keep the plant viable for longer. This extra period of viability will enable the foliage to generate surplus materials that are transferred to the bulbs which become that much larger and hence more likely to produce flowers the following season.

Pockets of stagnant water are invariably injurious to daffodil bulbs so great care should be taken when watering. Heavy applications need appropriate equipment if the pressure of the water is not to damage the foliage and impair its efficiency as the food factory of the plant. Overhead sprinkler systems which give a gentle spray are satisfactory, but need to be used for several hours to ensure that there is enough water to percolate down to the active roots. Systems of perforated plastic tubing can be laid amongst the plants to allow water to trickle into the soil, again the system should run for several hours to really wet the ground.

LIGHT

To be capable of manufacturing food reserves the daffodil leaves need the energy from sunlight to effect photosynthesis. Daffodils, once the shoots have emerged from the soil, do respond to light and in photoperiodism terms can be regarded as short day-plants. Photoperiodism, the study of plant reactions to varying intensities of light, has been of use in developing techniques for producing cut blooms and shows that the daffodil commences die-back as day lengths reduce. In open conditions growth will be maintained until the days begin to shorten. If there is an artificial shortening of day length by a reduction in the intensity of light the foliage may prematurely begin to lose viability. Thus, shade from overgrowth by deciduous trees/shrubs will reduce the cycle of growth and limit, unnecessarily, the future potential to produce flowers. It is sometimes argued that the daffodil has adapted to complete its cycle of bulb regeneration and development in the short period before it has to exist in the shadow cast by deciduous trees: this argument does not seem to recognise that shadeless hillside and mountain meadow environments are the natural homes of so many of the species.

Daffodils planted in heavy shade will, for one season, produce the flower which has developed in the bulb. The bulb substance will deteriorate and be only partially replenished as photosynthesis is not fully achieved. Partial replenishment will gradually reduce the size of the bulb until a flower cannot be sustained. Thus, bulbs planted in shade should be treated as annual bedding subjects and discarded after flowering or moved into a more favourable environment to recuperate for at least a couple of years.

COMPETITION WITH OTHER SUBJECTS

Due to their deep rooting system daffodils can reasonably successfully compete with other subjects and survive in most conditions. Where they are planted in borders or beds with shrubs, or a covering of other plants, developing foliage and flowers must not be impeded in their upward growth. Lateral growth of shrubs may mean that branches, roots and shoots cause physical damage to the daffodils, reducing the effectiveness of the display and perhaps eventually causing deterioration of the bulbs. Feeding of shrubs in a border will naturally be of initial benefit to interplanted daffodils but there will come a point when the rapidly developing roots of the shrubs will take most of nutrients from the soil. The ground near the bole of the shrub may well also be too dry for the effective growth of the daffodils. If they are competing with shrubs there needs to be a review of growth each spring to assess when movement of the bulbs is necessary to provide a more suitable environment.

Daffodils can and do exist quite happily under grass or shallow-rooted ground cover when planted at sufficient depth. Such surface coverings are not really in direct competition but the pattern of their growth may impede development of the shoots in the spring or cause their distortion. The major problem with such plantings is to ensure that the soil is kept sufficiently aerated to encourage growth. When bulbs are planted under grass, action needs to be taken to ensure that an impervious thatch is not created which limits the passage of water down to the roots; the scarifying of grass or aeration by forking will help. (See also page 54.)

Weeds amongst daffodils can be detrimental but in some situations they can be beneficial. Deep-rooted weeds cannot readily be removed without risk of damage to the daffodils and it is not always practicable to depend upon chemical treatments. A flush of weeds after the daffodils have flowered will keep light away from the foliage and may encourage its premature die-back. However, such a covering can help to reduce summer soil temperatures and create a more favourable environment for the dormant bulbs.

STAKING OF GROWTH

Healthy daffodil bulbs usually produce strong upright growth which does not need artificial support. Where conditions of growth are not ideal the foliage may be weak or excessively brittle and unable to stand erect on its own. It is rarely necessary to support each clump of leaves produced by a single bulb, and a few twigs or short canes and twine can be used to make a latticework cover through which the foliage can develop.

Some tall-growing hybrids, such as Sealing Wax (2Y-R), Bravoure (1W-Y) and Altruist (3O-R), or those which produce heavy heads, principally the doubles, such as Eastertide (4Y-Y), Unique (4W-Y) and Manly (4Y-O), are liable to topple over, especially after rain. This reduces the effectiveness of the display and can shorten its life. These cultivars should be given sufficient but unobtrusive support as they develop.

DEHEADING

Only a very small percentage of daffodil flowers will, left to natural agencies, set viable seed. However, where this does happen the plant will use a significant proportion of its food intake to sustain the developing seed at the expense of regeneration of the bulb. Unless seed is required from a chosen cross then the efficiency of the display of blooms in subsequent years will be improved by removing the flower-heads as soon as they fade.

This tedious operation will repay the effort involved. There is no one right way of doing it; the head can be removed with any conventional cutting tool or simply snapped off just below the spathe. It is preferable to make a clean cut so that the remaining stem is not damaged and can adopt the function of a leaf and, through photosynthesis, contribute to the build-up of the bulb.

It can be argued that if the vast majority of the flowers will not set seed then deheading is unnecessary; but in a garden setting there are two factors to be borne in mind. Firstly, even if seed has not been adequately fertilised the seedpod will inevitably swell, almost as if undergoing a false pregnancy, and this development takes reserves from the bulb. A pod may exist for three or four weeks before it decides to abort, and makes the stem top-heavy which increases the risk of breaking, near to the ground, and depriving the plant of a large proportion of its food-producing capacity. Secondly, the faded flower looks untidy and apart from acting as a wind vane can harbour diseases which may debilitate the plant (and can spread any virus present in the stock).

CARE OF FOLIAGE

Once broken off, flattened or otherwise damaged the daffodil leaf is not replaced. A fairly typical bulb will have four or five leaves and the flower stem so that loss of even one leaf will reduce the food-generating capacity by 16 to 20 per cent. This may not be a complete disaster but will limit the size of the bulb and in extreme cases means that the bulb is not large enough to produce a bloom in the following year.

After daffodils have flowered the 'tidy' gardener will resort to various practices to keep them looking neat. One often sees foliage tied into a knot, plaited or bent over and restrained with an elastic band. There is no doubt that such practices make the place look tended but the effect on the bulb is disastrous. It is equivalent to the discomfort experienced by tightening one's belt after a lavish dinner — but on a permanent basis. Toleration of a few weeks in which the foliage lacks geometric precision will inevitably result in a superior display in subsequent years.

PRECAUTIONARY SPRAYING

Purchase of stocks from reputable sources should mean that bulbs are free of disease. However, it is sensible to take precautionary measures to safeguard the health of established clumps of bulbs. Spraying of daffodil foliage, with a benomyl fungicide, when it is about 6in (15cm) tall and again after the flower-heads have been removed can do nothing but good.

FREQUENCY OF LIFTING

It is generally acknowledged that from time to time daffodil bulbs need lifting from the ground and replanting. Depending upon the situation in which the bulbs are growing, this process can be physically demanding and time consuming. It does, however, ensure that the ground under the bulbs can be enriched for the benefit of future displays and that overcrowded bulbs can be respaced to give better access to nutrients.

Many people agonise over the question of how frequently to lift their bulbs. There is no single correct answer to this question as so much will depend upon the particular purposes for which the grower is to use the daffodils. The major reasons for lifting bulbs can be summarised as:

- To check the health of the bulbs.
- To give them more space in which to develop.
- To make room for other subjects.
- To select suitable bulbs for special uses in the following season.

A grower may choose to lift the bulbs for a combination of these reasons, or for only one of them. For example, the exhibitor will be lifting to select the best bulbs for growing in pots or protected beds but will also take the opportunity to check that the bulbs are free from diseases or pests. Some people lift their bulbs every year; others may leave them in one place for so long that they fail to produce flowers because they are overcrowded and cannot obtain the necessary food from the impoverished soil. Best results can be obtained by a two- or three-year cycle of lifting, though much will depend upon the level of cultivation of the ground. Some naturalised bulbs never get lifted and apparently reach a sort of equilibrium with the natural manuring taking place, neither increasing nor decreasing.

In common with most exhibitors, I adopt the practice of lifting a number of bulbs of each cultivar each year, in careful rotation, so that some are available for use in pots. Where small off-sets have been planted they are usually left in the ground for two years so that they can build up to a good flowering size for the particular cultivar, but some larger bulbs may be left for only one year to the point where off-sets can be separated safely. However, the cultivars which are used for garden decoration are lifted only every three or four years unless the surrounding shrubs or perennials begin to overshadow them.

Timing is important: bulbs should be lifted, with great care being taken to avoid damaging them with either the fork or spade, just before the leaves are completely faded. This means that the remnants of the foliage mark the location of each bulb and its associated off-sets. Wherever possible the bulbs should be lifted from ground which is reasonably dry as this will mean that the soil falls away without the need for a lot of handling. In the ideal state the lifting will be done on a warm but cloudy day so that the bulbs are not exposed to the full power of direct sunlight, though they will not suffer too much if they get a limited period in full sunlight. The roughly-cleaned bulbs should be left to dry naturally to permit most of the soil and the foliage to be removed. They should then be placed in appropriate containers and carefully labelled, preferably with a permanent marker. (See also Chapter 2 on storage.)

MOVING 'IN-THE-GREEN'

It is generally regarded as preferable to move some plants whilst they are in growth, typical examples being snowdrops and certain cyclamen, but convention suggests that considerable damage will be caused if daffodils are moved except where they are in the period of apparent dormancy.

Most daffodils will survive being moved 'in-the-green' if this is done at the time of flowering or immediately after the flower fades. Care must be taken to limit damage to the roots when they are being lifted, and any damage to the foliage or flower stem must be avoided. There will be a limited regeneration of roots from the base-plate but there can be no replacement of the foliage. Any flower or its remains should be removed with as much of the stem, undamaged, as possible. When installed in their new quarters the bulbs should be planted slightly deeper, about 1 to 2in (2.5 to 5cm), with the soil being eased up to the foliage as a form of support.

Bulbs that have been moved 'in-the-green' should be regularly watered and will generally benefit from the application of liquid fertilisers. They may not flower the first year after the move, but they should gradually regain their vigour and be flowering normally after two or three years. Thus, the technique is a practical proposition and can be useful for removing 'rogue' cultivars from a stock or moving bulbs which may get swamped by overgrowth.

LABELLING OF CULTIVARS

The labelling of a border or bed of daffodils serves to identify where the bulbs are planted and as a reminder of which cultivar is in a particular location. The method depends on the individual gardener but as most daffodils remain in place for a minimum of one year, and perhaps several years, the labels should be long enough to stay securely in the soil. My own preference is for a 12in (30cm) length of $\frac{1}{2}$ by $\frac{3}{4}$in (1 by 2cm) wood at the back of which is attached a conventional 4in (10cm) plastic label. In the border the label is left out of sight except during the flowering season when it is rotated to an upright position for ready checking.

A wise precaution is to have a plan of the border recording the location of each cultivar. Such a planting plan can help to locate bulbs if labels become lost and can be useful when the gardener is deciding where extra cultivars can be fitted into the display to enhance its impact.

TIDYING UP

During the summer, foliage will begin to die back as the bulbs prepare for their storage function. Die-back will not be at the same time for every cultivar and will also be influenced by the conditions. The tips of the leaves will gradually turn brown and then whole leaves will yellow. If the bulbs are not being lifted the beds and borders need tidying up.

Clumps of leaves and remnants of the stems should be pulled cleanly away from the bulbs and gathered up. Daffodil foliage will rot down to produce good compost. However, disease spores will survive the composting process and subsequently spread across the garden, so for the health of all stocks it is safer to burn the foliage as soon as practicable or dispose of it as household refuse.

Once the foliage has been removed the beds and borders should have their surfaces well worked with a hoe to close the holes through which the foliage emerged. This action will help to conserve moisture at depth by preventing caking and cracking, and will also discourage some pests from travelling down the available holes to the bulb.

•4•
Daffodils for Special Effects

The true versatility of daffodils can best be appreciated by considering some of the marvellous displays that they can create, both in the home and in the garden.

Daffodils in pots and containers can be encouraged into flower and do bring an early spring into the home. Such displays will last for weeks and give the added thrill of watching the flowers actually develop. Thanks to commercial growing methods with applications of artificial heat and light, as well as the production of naturally early-flowering cultivars, cut daffodils are available for simple arrangements over some six months. Each display may retain its freshness for only a few days but during that time can give much pleasure. These arrangements can be varied by careful choice of different cultivars to give a range of perfumes to supplement the tremendous number of charming colour combinations.

Endless possibilities exist from the traditional mass plantings through to the unusual but delightful hanging baskets. There is inevitably some trial and error to establish the perfect cultural technique for a particular special effect but general pointers are given in the following sections.

MASS PLANTING

The sight of a solitary daffodil may stir some emotions, other than a feeling of pity, as we have become conditioned to the idea that the flowers should be in hosts or crowds. Perhaps we should really be concerned with planting in masses. Large and bold groupings of daffodils should be attempted whatever the size of the garden or growing space. Much more impact is achieved from twelve bulbs planted in a space of one square foot than can be attained from those same bulbs spaced one foot apart in a straight line.

To be successful over a number of years such a massed planting needs to have deeply dug ground which is free draining of water and to have a good dressing of a low-nitrogen fertiliser such as hoof and horn or bone meal incorporated below the bulbs. Very often the question arises 'Why have my daffodils not flowered this year when they gave such a wonderful display last year?' The answer is not easy but all of the indications are that there has been insufficient build-up of reserves within the bulbs. This can be due to foliage being flattened by winds, rain or snow, but more commonly it is lack of nutrients available in the soil. Massed plantings need good supplies of fertilisers each growing season but, because daffodils are taken for granted once planted, this fact is often forgotten. In a paddock or orchard some manuring may be available from livestock but may be insufficient. In borders or under trees, competition from other subjects may preclude enough of the fertiliser getting to the bulbs. A good general fertiliser, such as 'Vitax', should be applied to any area which is hosting a mass of daffodils and if the ground is dry, a liquid fertiliser, such as 'Chempak' or 'Phostrogen', would be advantageous.

Although traditionalists will always advocate the use of all-yellow flowers for such plantings, some quite spectacular effects can be produced with virtually any of the colour combinations. The all-white flowers attract a lot of attention and tend to be more brilliant, irrespective of the quality of the daylight. The red-cupped flowers, unless they are too closely examined and signs of burning are visible, are also dominant at most times. To really sparkle, the all-yellow flower appears to give its best display when it is seen in sunlight. Good effects can be achieved with three or four selected from Vigil (1W-W), Merlin (3W-YYR), Kingscourt (1Y-Y), Dove Wings (6W-Y), Trousseau (1W-Y), Sealing Wax (2Y-R) and Daydream (2Y-W) (see also Chapter 9). Clumps of one cultivar, for maximum impact, are therefore useful to provide splashes of colour or highlights early in the year.

Planting in mass can extend to the filling of formal island beds with daffodils. In this case allowances have to be made dependent upon what is to be planted in the bed for a summer display. To many people the work involved in emptying the bed after flowering and allowing time for some build-up of the bulbs is too much effort. Planting in this way usually means that new bulbs must be bought for the following year or that the original bulbs must be found some suitable ground in which to recuperate for a couple of years before being used again in a formal bed. With the present trend to smaller gardens this rest cycle is not always practicable. A better return can be obtained from the bulbs by a slightly deeper planting than would be considered normal, say 6 to 7in (15 to 18cm), so that over-planting can be effected by the summer bedding. However, even with this approach, every three or four years the bulbs will need to be dug from the bed so that they can be respaced with sufficient room to develop.

PLANTING IN GRASS

This approach is often regarded as the most natural-looking planting of daffodils and is usually referred to as naturalisation. It is true that many daffodils thrive and look well in grass though some of the species do not grow in such situations in their natural habitats.

If planting in grass is to be successful it must be accepted that a perfect sward cannot be achieved. It is impossible to cut the grass without cutting the daffodil foliage and in the interests of the developing bulb any cutting should be delayed until the bulb has had sufficient chance to regenerate itself to flowering size. Practical trials have clearly demonstrated that a minimum of six weeks must be allowed between the flowers fading and the grass, and foliage, being cut. Less than six weeks will mean a gradual annual deterioration of the bulbs and hence any display of blooms. More than six weeks will be beneficial but not significantly so compared with totally natural foliage die-back, usually achieved in about ten weeks. So-called 'naturalising mixtures' often contain a range of cultivars which flower over a three- or four-week time-scale and this means that the six-week period must be reckoned from the fading of the latest flowers.

Many retail outlets offer special naturalising mixtures of daffodils which may sound attractive and good value for money. It is unfortunate that the origins of such mixtures are extremely varied. In some cases they are bulbs that have been used for forcing, to produce early crops of cut flowers, which will need time to recuperate. Others are surplus stocks of named cultivars that have not been in great demand, and some may be seedling stocks that have not lived up to expectation after periods of trial. The results from such stock can be very uneven and can cause disappointments even though some splash of colour can be achieved.

More attractive displays can be obtained by planting individual cultivars in different areas as separate masses so that the attention moves from area to area as one cultivar fades and another is coming to its peak of perfection. Super effects can be achieved by using at least three of the cultivars identified above for mass planting but my favourites are Kingscourt (1Y-Y), Shining Light (2Y-ORR), Daydream (2Y-W) and Passionale (2W-P). A mixed group (which may have up to ten cultivars) in one area will probably have as long a total flowering period but never achieves maximum impact with some blooms fading before others open, or opening whilst others are barely buds. Separation of cultivars does mean that planted areas can be tidied up on a progressive basis so that some gradual improvements can be seen — it has a wonderful psychological effect.

Even for those on a very limited budget there are many cultivars that are eminently suited to planting in grass. The principle of separation of cultivars means that the total area to be planted can be subdivided and tackled bit by bit over a number of years until the desired effect is achieved. It also means that cultivars can be chosen appropriate to the ground conditions. Species, usually having smaller bulbs, can be used where the soil is relatively shallow and the various forms of N *bulbocodium* or N *cyclamineus* will respond well and give an interesting colour effect: they may also set seed and give a two-fold method of increase over a number of years. Very free draining soil which gets a good summer baking would be more suited to the tazettas and jonquils. In other situations the fibre/humus content of the soil may be more appropriate to the near-wild forms such as Van Sion, the Lent lily and the Tenby daffodil.

The degree of exposure of a site can also influence the choice of cultivars. It is most unrewarding to plant tall-growing cultivars in an exposed area or in a natural wind tunnel. Staking is not a practical proposition for large planting in grass and the tall stems will be prone to breakage. Fortunately some of the miniatures and near-miniatures can give a good response in such situations and because of the shortness of their stems avoid unnecessary breakages.

The range of options is therefore very wide. Time spent experimenting with one or two bulbs of a number of cultivars is not wasted and will ultimately result in a far better display than can be achieved by planting a naturalising mixture which may not be appropriate to your conditions.

Bulbs naturalised in grass should inevitably be seen as a long-term project. They are not easy to plant where grass is already established nor are they easy to remove if the result is not pleasing or they have become overcrowded. Naturalised bulbs should be given sufficient space in which to develop, at least 12in (30cm) between each one. It is preferable to plant each bulb as a complete unit and not to remove off-sets, so that a natural-looking growth is established even in the first season. Where groups of one cultivar are being planted it is essential to create an irregular outline to the clump and irrespective of the chosen basic shape there should be a point, off-centre, which has the greatest concentration, with a thinning-out to the edges.

It is best to remove the turf over the intended area so that the ground can be well worked and enriched with some fertiliser. The bulbs can then be positioned and covered with the soil and the turf relaid or grass seed sown. If this task is impossible, individual holes should be dug with a trowel or spade, or one of the special bulb planters. There are many different bulb planters, but they all remove a round core of soil to create a hole in which the bulb can be placed. They are useful for planting small bulbs but do not produce the diameter or depth of hole to cope with large multi-nosed bulbs. Although it is a tedious operation, great benefit is gained by loosening the soil at the base of each hole and incorporating a little fertiliser.

In the spring, areas of grass which have been underplanted with daffodils must be kept free of traffic. Walking across the grass may be a temptation but can cause damage to the daffodil shoots even though they may still be below the surface. Even more serious damage can be caused if the shoots are trodden down when they are 3 to 4in (7.5 to 10cm) tall as the flower-buds will be above the surface. After flowering, if there is sufficient space to move through the planted area, some attempt to dehead the stems should be made. If there is a risk of damaging the foliage it is wiser to forget the deheading. Until the foliage dies back and can be trimmed off, walking across the planted area can cause damage which will affect the bulbs' ability to regenerate. Once the grass has been trimmed off there should be no risk of damage to the bulbs until the following spring.

Grass which has been underplanted with daffodils will benefit from regular maintenance and in particular the application of appropriate fertilisers in autumn and spring. The majority of such fertilisers will be absorbed by the grass but inevitably some will be transported down to a depth where it can be absorbed by the roots of the daffodils. Chemical treatment aimed at soil pests and diseases or at weeds should be used only when there is no daffodil foliage above the soil surface. This, to be absolutely sure, means avoiding their use between midwinter and midsummer. The only exception, for the average planting, would be the application of benomyl to treat fungal disease after the daffodils have flowered — this chemical can help to eliminate diseases which are specific to daffodils.

TROUGHS, POTS AND WINDOW BOXES

Such containers are ideal for creating a splash of colour where it can be most appreciated or have maximum impact. Unless the trough, pot or window box is extremely large, and hence immovable, it is unlikely to have sufficient depth to allow the daffodils to have a natural root development. This means that the best results are obtained where the bulbs are planted for one season and are effectively treated as annuals.

The bulbs, from a specialist supplier or from stocks grown in the garden, should be planted about four weeks later than would be the practice for conventional beds or borders (see page 46). This extra period of storage needs careful management to keep the bulbs in condition but should mean that they are not planted into a container that is to suffer wide fluctuations of temperature. If spare containers are available they can be planted in early autumn provided they can be stood in a cool, sheltered position which reduces the risk of temperature variations. Ideally, spare containers should be plunged in peat to give a total depth of covering over the bulbs of 4in (10cm) for standard cultivars and $1\frac{1}{2}$in (4cm) for miniatures.

The drainage in the containers must be adequate to prevent water pockets building up. Such trapped water is likely to freeze and squash the life out of young roots or at least mean that they are permanently flooded and unable to function.

The choice of cultivars is really only influenced by the potential problems of wind damage. The lower-growing cultivars, such as Tête-à-Tête (6Y-O),

Some effective combinations are:

- A centre of Dove Wings (6W-Y) surrounded by *Scilla siberica*, giving a sparkling blue edge to the delicate colouring of the daffodils.
- A centre of Loch Owskeich (2Y-O) surrounded by Charity May (6Y-Y), giving a mound of clear yellow topped by the intensely-coloured çoronas of the taller-growing hybrid.
- A centre of Charity May (6Y-Y) surrounded by Tête-à-Tête (6Y-O), a nice low grouping, ideal for a windy area, of varying shades of yellow. Gives a long-lasting display.
- A planting of Kingscourt (1Y-Y) growing through forget-me-nots, giving a delicate cloud of blue that enhances the golden yellow of the daffodil.
- A planting of Geranium (8W-O) edged with *Tulipa fosterina*, being an interesting combination of white and orange shades that sparkles on a sunny day and is highly perfumed.

Hawera (5Y-Y) and Minnow (8W-Y), are less liable to damage and will not cause such a restriction of visibility past a window box. The greatest impact is created by having the entire contents of the container in flower at one time. This can be achieved by planting only one cultivar in the container, or by careful choice of two cultivars known to flower at the same time with a shorter one acting as an edging, or by use of one cultivar edged with another genus that will flower at the same time. If another genus is used it may be planted across the surface of the container so that its stems and leaves act as a support for the daffodils.

The use of daffodils with distinctive perfumes can give an added impact to the containers: Minnow (8W-Y), Geranium (8W-O) and Erlicheer (4W-W) are super when used in this way.

Once the flowers have faded the container should be cleared in preparation for the next display. If the bulbs are regarded as expendable they should be disposed of by burning or including with household refuse. If they are to be retained they can be removed with as much soil attached as is practicable and planted in a hole in a sheltered part of the garden to die back naturally, though they may take two or three years to regain full vigour. If there are spare containers to accommodate the next display, the daffodils should be kept watered and fed until they die back naturally. Plastic baskets, as used for aquatic plants, can be of value in combination with other types of container: they can be planted and plunged to get good root development and be transferred to the containers in early winter to be removed and replunged after

A SELECTION OF CULTIVARS raised in the United States of America by Grant E. Mitsch whose daffodil breeding extended over a period of fifty years. *Top left* Executive (2Y-Y) (1972); *top right* Grebe (4Y-O) (1979); *centre* Honeybird (1Y-W) (1965); *bottom left* Pasteline (2W-P) (1979); *bottom right* Gold Frills (3W-WWY) (1966)

(*overleaf*) DAYDREAM (2Y-W) makes a superb, long lasting display when grown in a border. It is also still a good show cultivar

flowering. In this way the majority of the roots will not be damaged and the bulbs will complete an almost natural cycle of growth.

Containers need to be given regular attention to ensure that the compost or soil is not allowed to dry out. Regular watering as the flower-buds develop will allow them to expand to their maximum potential and they will last that much longer. A weak solution of liquid fertiliser (preferably high in potash) once a week will also be of benefit.

HANGING BASKETS

Traditionally, hanging baskets are regarded as a summer ornamentation. With a little patience and attention to detail it is possible to create very pleasant spring displays in which daffodils feature prominently. This approach has become more practicable with the greater availability of the miniature types of daffodil, especially those that carry a number of flowers on each stem, such as Hawera (5Y-Y), April Tears (5Y-Y), Tête-à-Tête (6Y-O) and Minnow (8W-Y).

Wire baskets are more suitable for growing daffodils than some of the modern plastic containers as it is easier to obtain a more rounded effect.

Miniatures are especially effective where a number have been allowed to grow through the sides of the basket. They will provide a good density of blooms from one layer of bulbs and this can permit the use of contrasting subjects on the second layer to create multi-coloured displays. Short-growing larger cultivars, such as Vigil (1W-W), Daydream (2W-Y), Rippling Waters (5W-W) and Liberty Bells (5Y-Y), can also be grown successfully in baskets.

Shaped terracotta pots designed for hanging on walls can also be used for daffodils but again it is important to ensure that they are planted sufficiently early and are plunged in a cool sheltered spot through until early spring. These pots must be wrapped in newspaper prior to being plunged to save the chore of cleaning them when they are lifted. Once lifted the climatic conditions may not be suitable for them to be immediately located on the wall and they should be kept in a protected environment so that the compost does not become frozen. Try to avoid hanging these pots where they will be exposed to rapid variations of temperature — direct sunlight later in the day is preferable.

CULTIVARS WHICH ARE POPULAR FOR EXHIBITION and garden decoration — all raised in England. *Top centre* Kimmeridge (3W-YYO) from D. Blanchard; *top left* Strines (2Y-Y) from F. E. Board; *top right* April Love (1W-W) from Mrs Abel Smith; *centre* Shining Light (2Y-OOR) from F. E. Board; *bottom left* Broomhill (2W-W) from F. E. Board; *bottom right* Golden Vale (Y-Y) from F. E. Board

Growing in wire baskets. The technique is relatively simple to set up; the important stages are as follows:

1 Ensure that the basket has a good compacted layer of sphagnum moss, about 1in (2.5cm) thick.
2 Position a few bulbs so that their noses are almost through the moss and about half-way down the sides of the basket.
3 Put a layer of good, free-draining soil or compost across the base of the basket and gently compress it.
4 Space bulbs across the compost and fill the spaces between them with more compost so that the tips of the bulbs are still identifiable.
5 Space a second layer of bulbs on the compost and between the tips of the original layer.
6 Fill the spaces between the bulbs with compost and ensure that the basket is filled to within ½in (1cm) of the top.
7 Plunge the filled basket under a 4in (10cm) layer of peat in a sheltered spot that does not get direct sunlight and keep it well watered.
8 In early spring remove the basket from the plunge and stand on an inverted plant pot in a greenhouse or conservatory. Keep the basket well watered and rotate it through 90 degrees in the same direction each day.
9 As the buds begin to break the basket can be hung outside in a prominent position. If severe protracted frosts are experienced the basket may need to be moved inside at night.

COLOUR IN THE HOME

Daffodils can be used to create a variety of decorative effects in the home. It is never possible for them to complete their full cycle of growth in a protected indoor environment, especially where central heating is used, but by careful manipulation they can be brought inside to allow their full beauty, and perfume, to be enjoyed for ten to fourteen days whilst at their peak of performance. Provided this period indoors is only brief the bulbs can be saved from too much deterioration. And in this way we can get a lot of pleasure from close association with the blooms and delude ourselves that spring is really on the way.

With the range of cultivars generally available, one can choose to display them in any way from bold colourful arrangements to tiny table centrepieces. Cost may well influence choice: 50p per bulb sounds expensive but a suitable container of just five bulbs will give a splendid return if flowered in early spring. The flowers will last about two weeks and represent better value than the equivalent expenditure on cut blooms that may not reach full potential and will have a much shorter life. With suitable care after the period in the home the majority of bulbs can be retained to give many years of bloom in the garden. However, prepared bulbs designed for Christmas flowering need special attention as detailed later.

There is little doubt that conventional plant pots (either clay or plastic) provide the most suitable conditions for indoor daffodils, especially in the

HAWERA (5Y-Y), a delightful triandus hybrid growing about 8in (20cm) tall. It is now widely available and is useful in pots, window boxes and hanging baskets; on a rockery it makes a long-lasting display of colour

avoidance of water-logged compost. Plant pots can of course be stood inside decorative containers of plastic, porcelain, pewter etc to improve the appearance of the display but this outer container must not be allowed to fill with water. Bowls, of porcelain, china or pottery, which do not have drainage holes can be used quite successfully for daffodils provided that a special bulb fibre is used and it is not excessively watered, but kept damp.

Whichever type of container is used the best display will be achieved by packing as many bulbs as possible into it. If a limited number of bulbs are available, reduce the size of the container to keep the anticipated flowers in proportion. It is possible, using standard plant pots, to plant the bulbs in two layers to enhance the volume of flower: by a peculiar quirk of nature all of the flowers will be produced at a fairly uniform height above the pot. A 6in (15cm) pot can accommodate six fairly large bulbs in two layers provided they are not planted directly on top of one another.

Using plant pots, the bulbs should be planted in a John Innes type compost as early in the autumn as possible and should be covered except for their noses. Miniatures, especially species, should be fully covered with at least ¾in (2cm) of compost. The pots should be plunged under a 4in (10cm) layer of peat or soil for about twelve weeks to encourage good development of the roots and initiation of growth of the leaves and flower-buds. If decorative pots are used they can be kept clean by being wrapped in newspaper before being plunged; the shoots of the bulbs will grow through the paper once it has softened with moisture from the plunge. Lifting of pots from the plunge can take place any time after the twelve weeks have elapsed, subject only to the covering material not being frozen. If early lifting is planned, alternatives to plunging under peat or soil may be appropriate. These will depend upon facilities available, but the pots should be kept in a cool, dark environment where wide fluctuations of temperature can be avoided. Air must be able to circulate: a dark, cool, airy cellar is preferable to a closed, cold cupboard. A corner of the garden which is in permanent heavy shade may be suitable provided the containers get adequate water to stimulate the bulbs. Miniatures must not be plunged in too deep a covering of material. A covering in excess of 1in (2.5cm) will result in drawn growth which is unable to support itself and requires excessive staking to the detriment of the display.

Once lifted, the containers can be brought into the house. Initially they still require very cool conditions whilst the shoots develop their proper green colouring and to avoid excessive elongation of leaves. Too high a temperature, anything over 55°F (13°C), can cause the flower-buds to abort and spoil the display. As growth proceeds, temperatures during the day can be increased to advance the flowers but too much 'forcing' can produce leaf growth at a faster rate than stem growth, again reducing the efficiency of the display. Good light is important at all times once the leaves have turned green if even growth is to be achieved. Pots should not be left in one position but partly rotated each day so that the developing flowers are on upright stems and give an all-round display. With the standard cultivars, even the shorter-growing ones, it may be advantageous to insert a single split cane into the centre of the pot to which loops of green or black twine or thin wool can be fixed. Such loops can gradually slide up the split cane to give support to the foliage and stems. The system of tying needs to be as unobtrusive as possible. Once it is clear that the flower-stems have reached their ultimate height (the neck will bend) the split cane can be cut so that it is not visible above the flowers.

After the flowers have passed their best, if the bulbs are regarded as expend-able they should be discarded immediately as household refuse. Pots which have been crammed full of bulbs will be unable to sustain them and so, if you wish to keep them, at the first available opportunity the whole clump together with the compost should be taken out of the pot and planted into the garden. If there is little disturbance of the clump the roots of the bulbs will range into the soil in search of nutrients — such clumps will benefit from regular watering with liquid fertiliser. The clumps can be left in position to give further displays in subsequent years or they can be lifted, once the foliage has died back, for replanting with more appropriate spacings between the bulbs. Some pots, particularly those of miniatures, will have sufficient com-post to allow reasonable growth to take place, and they can be stood in a sheltered spot and kept watered and fed until the foliage dies back naturally. Except for some miniatures, especially the smaller species, bulbs which have been used in this way need a recuperation period of one or two years to get back to full size.

Where bowls without drainage holes are preferred the techniques are very similar. Special bulb fibre must be used as this with its shell and charcoal content does not go stale even if a shallow layer of water is retained under the bulbs. A layer of bulb fibre about 1½in (4cm) should be placed in the bottom of the bowl and the bulbs stood upright on this. The spaces between the bulbs should be filled with more bulb fibre without excessive compaction. The noses will inevitably show above the compost if a small allowance is left at the top of the bowl to facilitate watering. As soon as it is planted the con-tainer should be watered and after about one hour it should be tipped onto its side to allow excess water to drain off. Plunging of this type of container will inevitably lead to waterlogging and so it should be stored in a very cool, dark, airy place for about twelve weeks. During this period it should be checked once a week to ensure that the bulb fibre is sufficiently moist and watered as appropriate. After each watering the container should be tipped onto its side to allow any excess water to drain off.

When bowls are brought into the light they need the same care and attention as for conventional plant pots of daffodils. Watering will still require special consideration. If it is necessary to give some support to the foliage, and a wire support or patent device was not incorporated at the time of planting, a split cane with twine loops should be used. However, the soft, relatively shallow bulb fibre will not hold the cane rigidly enough and it will have to be speared into one of the bulbs at the centre of the container. This will not cause irreparable damage to the bulb and will enable the tying-up arrangement to be neat and inconspicuous.

After the flowers have faded any bulbs which are to be retained for future years should be planted in the garden. The complete clump of bulbs and fibre should be buried under at least 3in (7.5cm) of soil which must be carefully worked between the groups of leaves. They should be watered regularly with liquid fertiliser until they die back naturally. It is preferable to lift these bulbs and replant them at appropriate spacings as this ensures that the bulb fibre does not stay as a sponge and is incorporated into the soil.

CHRISTMAS DAFFODILS

In the northern hemisphere, with Christmas falling in the dark days of winter it is possible to have a foretaste of spring with some daffodils as a floral decoration. Commercial cut flower suppliers have developed special forcing techniques to ensure that a limited number of cultivars are in bloom. However, much more interest can be created by having some daffodils flowering in pots or containers.

There are two ways of achieving daffodils in flower at Christmas. Clones which normally bloom in midwinter, such as Nylon (12W-W), a charming bulbocodium, can be grown outdoors in pots and brought into the home once in flower. Alternatively, specially prepared bulbs can be obtained.

Prepared bulbs are fairly readily available, usually in early autumn, in a limited range of cultivars, the most widely known being Paperwhite Grandiflora (8W-W) and Grand Soleil d'Or (8Y-O). These bulbs have been stored in very carefully controlled conditions to encourage the development of the embryo flower and do not require an additional period of cool dark conditions. Usually the growers have carefully selected the bulbs prior to treating them so that they are of a fairly uniform size and capable of producing a flower. Hence, apart from checking for any signs of excessive softness no special care is needed when buying these bulbs.

The usual cultivation system is to support the bulbs in an upright position on a 1½in (4cm) layer of washed gravel in a decorative container without drainage holes. The spaces between the bulbs are then filled with gravel and the whole is watered. Water should not fill the container and should not rise to the base of the bulbs. The container can stand in a cool room in good light,

PAPERWHITE GRANDIFLORA (8W-W) is extremely popular and reliable for an early indoor display of daffodils and has the bonus of a heady perfume. Specially-prepared bulbs, once planted in decorative bowls which are an integral part of the display, can be grown on a cool windowsill

say on a window sill, and should be rotated gradually to encourage even, upright development. From the moment of watering the bulbs it is the temperature and intensity of light which will determine the timing of the flowers. To get an extended display do not plant all the bulbs at once but have two or three containers planted up at ten-day intervals. Any bulbs not to be planted immediately should be kept cool and dry. If developing plants are exposed to temperatures in excess of 60°F (16°C) they may become drawn and have weak stems, though they can be tied up in the same way as bulbs grown in bulb fibre. At high temperatures some of the flower buds may abort.

These prepared bulbs become very weakened by this system of growth. Attempts can be made to retain them though the climate may not be compatible with their requirements: most of these cultivars need a hot climate to give a good summer baking and indeed most of the bulbs on sale in the UK now originate from Israel. Once they have flowered they are better discarded.

Naturally early cultivars, such as untreated Grand Soleil d'Or (8Y-O) or Rijnveld's Early Sensation (1Y-Y), should be treated as other pot or container grown cultivars and if planted in late summer they can be brought inside after ten weeks of cool growth. Manipulation of light and heat will then encourage the blooms to develop but the system is not entirely reliable in terms of being able to time the blooms for perfection by Christmas.

IN THE CONSERVATORY/GREENHOUSE

Displays of daffodils can be created in such protected environments using slight variations on the techniques described above. Their impact requires variations of height that can be achieved by stepped staging or by the use of cultivars which have different natural heights. Post-flowering attention to the pots is important if the bulbs are to be retained. The environment should encourage the plants to have a growth cycle as near natural as possible, and watering, with liquid fertilisers incorporated, should be undertaken regularly until the foliage begins to fade.

There are some cultivars which give of their best only in a conservatory or greenhouse. The tazettas and jonquils can be brought into flower that much earlier than would be the case in the open ground and their perfumes can be appreciated to the full. After flowering cultivars from these two groupings will respond well if kept under protection and once their foliage begins to fade they should not receive further water. However, the pots should be kept in full sun so that they really dry out and the bulbs get the essential baking which will help to induce flowers in the following season.

CUT FLOWERS

Daffodils are popular florists' flowers and through imports, forcing and seasonal variations can be available for five or six months of the year. Over the years there has been a change in the style of marketing cut blooms. Currently most daffodils are cut at the pencil-bud stage which means that the flowers develop with the ultimate purchaser. The growers therefore have to select cultivars that develop well in water even though full potential size is rarely achieved. Though it is difficult to define more than the perianth colour at the time the flowers are bought it does mean that the developing blooms can be appreciated over a longer period. Packaging and hence transport costs are contained by this method of marketing and help keep retail prices at reasonable levels. Experimental work is still being undertaken to try to find and develop cultivars with longer and better vase life so that cut blooms will be even better value for money.

When they are cut from the plant daffodil stems and foliage excrete a colourless slime or sap. This does not appear to affect the vase life of daffodils but can cause other types of flower to die prematurely; this is especially true of irises which are popular companions in floral displays. Fortunately, cut daffodils, after a period of about three hours standing in cold water, cease to exude this slime even if further cuts are made to their stems, so to get the best return daffodils should stand alone for a while before being used in mixed arrangements. A square cut across the stem to the desired length will be satisfactory where they are to be displayed on a pin-holder or in a conventional vase. However, where floral foam is used as the base of the display the stems should be cut at a steep angle to help them penetrate the foam. Forced flowers usually have quite weak stems and should not be forced into the foam — first prepare a hole using a skewer or length of suitable garden cane.

With their angular heads and straightness of stem daffodils are not the easiest of flowers to use in floral arrangements. Indeed, many people fight shy of trying to use them, but there are a number of ways in which their features can be highlighted. For example, in a straight-sided glass container the varying greens of the stems can make an attractive contribution to the overall display. Too much arrangement of individual blooms should be avoided and any variation in stem length should be quite small.

Within any bunch of daffodils there are usually some that are more advanced. This graduation in size can be used to good effect in a modern, angular arrangement in a shallow container. Various shaped leaves and foliage can be used to mask the 'mechanics' be it floral foam or pin-holder. A softness of outline can be achieved by a background framework of bare twigs, catkins or early-flowering shrub material such as flowering currant (*Ribes sanguineum*). The association of new foliage growth and daffodils clearly indicates the coming spring and always attracts attention.

Traditional triangular arrangements of daffodils with other spring subjects, such as iris and tulip, are successful where there are enough blooms to give a very full effect. Such arrangements need a substantial stemmed container to give the correct balance. Large blooms, especially the modern doubles including Unique (4W-Y), Eastertide (4Y-Y) and Manly (4Y-O), are ideal for emphasising the central focal point of the display against the frame of new foliage, the in-filling being smaller flowers of some of the multi-headed cultivars from the jonquilla types such as Sweetness (7Y-Y) or Dickcissel (7Y-W).

Pedestal displays can be extremely successful using one cultivar, or a mixture of cultivars, or a mix of daffodils and other subjects. Because these displays are relatively large and will be viewed from a distance, the placing of colour is important. It must be remembered that the back of a daffodil bloom is just as colourful as the front and from a distance will not look out of place. Many modern cultivars do produce fairly long stems so that a full cascade effect can be achieved. Good subjects are Acropolis (4W-R), Sealing Wax (2Y-R), Merlin (3W-YYR) or Altruist (3O-R).

Table centrepieces can be created using the miniature cultivars in appropriate-sized containers. Splendid effects can be obtained with Little Gem (1Y-Y), Segovia (3W-Y), Minnow (8W-Y) or Hawera (5Y-Y). Obviously any foliage or other material used must be in keeping with both the size of the display and the size of the daffodils. Some cultivars, for example Erlicheer (4W-W) or N jonquilla (1OY-Y), whilst they are attractive have perfumes which do not appeal to everyone and may be inappropriate on the dining table.

IN THE ROCK GARDEN

Elaborate rock gardens are rarely built today and could not be accommodated in the average plot. However, many gardeners try to create small-scale versions, such as raised beds to accommodate a wide range of plants. Such beds with their edgings and arrangement of stones can be filled with varying soil mixtures to suit the requirements of different plants, and daffodils can be included in the whole. Raised-bed styles of rock garden give good drainage, especially where grit, gravel or stone chippings are incorporated, which is to the liking of many of the miniature daffodils and in particular some of the species. Surface dressing of the rock garden with stone chippings will help deter slugs which are usually attracted to the foliage of miniature daffodils. Space should really be found for N cyclamineus, the bulbocodiums and N triandus albus as well as Little Gem (1Y-Y), Little Sentry (7Y-Y) and Clare (7Y-Y) as a minimum.

Dependent upon the scale of the rock garden it may be advantageous to include some of the taller-growing cultivars to help give variation. Ensure that taller-growing subjects do not create shadow for other plants and that their foliage does not become flattened onto smaller subjects and cause distortion to their growth. Good cultivars are detailed in Chapter 9 but splendid displays should include Dove Wings (6W-Y), Foundling (6W-P), Liberty Bells (5Y-Y) and Jet Fire (6Y-R).

Each cultivar, or species, should be planted as a separate clump to give maximum impact. In this style of garden the number of bulbs constituting each clump is not too important. Indeed, a single bulb of a scarce cultivar may cause as much excitement as a hundred of an easy grower and may get cosseted to encourage it to multiply.

N triandus albus (10W-W), affectionately known as Angel's Tears, is a charming and robust species. It performs extremely well in the rock garden, and in pots in a cool greenhouse. The pendant flowers are one of the characteristics transmitted to cultivars which are classified as triandus hybrids, Division 5

•5•
Growing for Exhibition

Spring flower shows are becoming major events in the programmes arranged by local horticultural societies and are splendid opportunities for members to get together and create a public interest in gardening generally. Growing for exhibition is not too difficult and it is a test of your cultivation skills and your ability to present well-prepared exhibits for assessment. We all like to think that we can grow blooms as well as our neighbour but it is still a thrill to have an expert judge endorse our personal opinion. Of greater importance is the creation of a comprehensive display of modern daffodils which can encourage other people to extend the range of cultivars which they grow. The more people that participate the greater the spectacle, and winning is a bonus.

A daffodil bulb of sufficient size will generally produce a flower when grown with a reasonable amount of care and attention. The season of growth can significantly affect the perfection of the finished flower and good management can have a major influence upon its quality as assessed in relation to size, texture and, to a lesser extent, its colouring. Growing for exhibition is a combination of skills: those for producing good-quality bulbs and those for producing blooms to the peak of perfection on the appointed date.

In the season leading up to the show the cultural regime is therefore aimed at maximising the potential of the bloom already within the bulb by attempting to ensure that at all stages of growth the developing flower is provided with conditions which are correctly matched to the demands of the plant. An additional important consideration is the need to ensure that the forces of nature realistically expected in a typical spring do not create damage that will detract from the full beauty of the bloom. A large part of the growing for exhibition is a serious concern for suitable protection of the bloom so that it will be presented on the show-bench in as perfect condition as possible.

Different cultivars respond in different ways to specialised cultural systems and the only way to find out about these preferences is to experiment. There are in essence two basic systems of growing for exhibition — in pots or in the 'open' ground — and most exhibitors find that they have to be used as complementary systems to give a full range of cultivars for specific dates. There are advantages and disadvantages to both systems and the degree of priority given to each will depend upon the location and its normal climate, and the finances available to purchase the bits and pieces of equipment needed to get the best results.

It is a prerequisite of growing for exhibition that suitable bulbs of the cultivars, appropriate to the level of competition being contemplated, are readily available. A study of show schedules will identify what is required for particular exhibits (see Chapter 6). Major collection classes at a national show will require cultivars that have the inbuilt style, form and colours to give blooms that should get good points scores. Price limit classes are restrictive in the range of cultivars which can be utilised but some cultivars are much more reliable than others and therefore more likely to give a high proportion of blooms that will do well.

All this implies that there needs to be some planning of what is to be planted and in what conditions to ensure that a sufficient range of cultivars is grown in anticipation of being able to enter a particular class or classes. For example, to produce entries for the Daffodil Society's deNavarro Cup class, requiring twelve cultivars — three stems of each from not less than three divisions — I have usually by the midsummer of the previous year identified twenty-four cultivars of which an adequate supply of good bulbs is likely to be available and from which I could expect a minimum of ten good blooms of each cultivar to make the final selection. Such a selection could be achieved from six bulbs of Unique (4W-Y) or ten bulbs of Merlin (3W-YYR) or twenty bulbs of Arctic Gold (1Y-Y). To be fully effective planning needs to be based on full records of how particular cultivars have performed in previous seasons. In assessing the number of bulbs the aim is to have a uniformity of

---

Pot culture:
Advantages — pots can be moved around to ensure that blooms develop uniformly;
— can be moved from location to location to advance or retard the blooms;
— can be fed and watered as appropriate to the needs of the particular cultivar.

Disadvantages
— high initial cost of pots and shelter;
— colour and texture of blooms can be adversely affected by the intensity of sunlight through glass and the micro-climate within the shelter;
— bulbs can, unless well tended, take two years to recover from a season in pots.

'Open' ground:
Advantages
— generally gives a better colouring of bloom and smoother texture;
— bulbs do not need to recover but retain their ability to flower as conditions have been near to normal;
— requires less physical effort day to day.

Disadvantages
— very difficult to advance or retard blooms on the plant;
— some white perianths never really whiten;
— individual cultivars cannot be given specific attention.

size and type, assuming that a show-sized bloom will be obtained from either a large round bulb or a good double-nosed bulb. A simple system will note the conditions under which each cultivar was grown, what was cut for exhibition on particular days, what could have been cut, what was actually staged and the results achieved.

Aiming to make a final selection from ten blooms of a particular cultivar may sound excessive. However, the ten blooms will not be at identical stages of development on a given day. They may have size and/or colour variations which will make it difficult to balance three blooms in as many respects as possible. If there are enough potential blooms the grower can risk advancing some of them to make sure that the cultivar is at least available for consideration. So there is no implication here that my system has to take account of inconsistent cultivars but the suggestion, based on experience, is that additional options are kept open.

Most keen exhibitors will regularly purchase new cultivars to enhance their collections with a view to competing at progressively higher levels. Suggestions for cultivars are given in Chapter 9. It is a fairly common practice that such new purchases are, at least for their first season, grown in pots — the hope being that a show standard bloom may be obtained but also to have the blooms more accessible for contemplation and appreciation. This practice has its uses but means that the cultivar takes longer to become acclimatised to its new environment and may not give a true reflection of its full potential. However, it also means that new stocks are to some extent in isolation and any risk of cross-infection is minimised.

There are a number of cultivars which are generally only available as pre-cooled/treated bulbs. Paperwhite Grandiflora or Grand Soleil d'Or are useful and popular cultivars for early displays but in the pre-cooled state they cannot be used successfully for exhibition. Thus, these types of bulbs should be avoided.

CUT BLOOMS FROM POTS

Production of cut flowers from pot-grown bulbs is often very hard work as each pot may have to be moved from place to place a number of times during a season of growth. It may save some work in terms of the effort needed to protect blooms from the elements but of course it is not a system to which all cultivars respond equally satisfactorily.

In general terms, cultivars with white, or whitish, perianths tend to do well in pots and of course the additional protection which is afforded in a glass-house or equivalent keeps the blooms free of dust and dirt. Thus, there is less need for grooming and hence less risk of bruising the flower. Some yellow perianth cultivars can be persuaded to do reasonably well in pots though they generally lack substance and can lose some of the intensity of colouring with the additional warmth that generally accompanies protection. Cultivars with intense colouring in the corona produce additional problems — some of them are inclined to burn or fade in sunlight in any event, so that the intensification and filtering effect of glass can magnify the extent of such damage. Against these generalisations the protection requirements of each cultivar will influence what needs to be done to get a nicely finished bloom. The cultural regime will be fairly standard to each grower but experience of the likes and dislikes of each cultivar may necessitate minor variations.

The first requirement after the supply of bulbs is an adequate supply of pots. Traditionally, there is a preference for clay pots and where these are already available they are first class. However, because clay is porous moisture evaporates fairly rapidly through the sides of the pot. As daffodils require abundant supplies of water, particularly at flowering time, there is not the same advantage in using clay pots as when growing, say, chrysanthemums, which do not like their roots too wet. Plastic pots are much cheaper than clay ones of the same size and they are very much lighter to carry round, both points to be remembered if a large number of pots are to be used. The one disadvantage is that, because there is no evaporation through plastic pots, if they are struck by direct sunlight they can produce too warm a compost that will result in damage to the bulbs.

Of greater importance than the material of the pot is the size if there is to be a sufficient root run to encourage the bulbs to develop as well as is possible for the following season. Half pots may be appropriate for growing for display purposes but for exhibition blooms full-depth pots are a must.

Final decisions on the size of pot to adopt will depend upon the quality of bulbs available at planting time. It is always better to err on the generous side. The number of bulbs of a miniature for a 5in (12cm) pot could be significantly increased but by restricting it to five each bloom will be well spaced from its neighbour and the bulbs will complete an almost normal cycle of growth.

Ideally, planting should be on the basis of one cultivar per pot. Mixing of cultivars may reduce the number of pots required but unless the two cultivars can be guaranteed to flower at the same time the facility to manipulate the time of flowering is significantly reduced when balancing the conflicting demands.

The following gives a guide to the number of bulbs that can be accommodated in different sizes of pot:

Diameter

10in + (25cm) 4 or 5 double-nosed bulbs

9in (22cm): 3 double-nosed or 4 to 5 round bulbs

7in (17cm): 2 double-nosed or 3 round bulbs

5in (12cm): up to 5 bulbs of a miniature

Everyone would like to have a large supply of bulbs from which to select those to be grown in pots — but this is rarely practicable. It is generally accepted that large round bulbs are most likely to produce top-quality blooms and hence these should be the first choice for growing in pots. A tightly-clustered double-nosed bulb will probably produce two blooms but they are likely to be of different sizes. Such bulbs can take up more room in pots and their variable return must be allowed for. However, some cultivars, for example Arkle (1Y-Y) or Tudor Minstrel (2W-Y), produce a more refined bloom from the secondary growth. Multi-nosed bulbs may not yield any greater number of blooms though there will be a much greater number of leaves trying to draw food through the roots for photosynthesis and the rate of development of the off-sets is likely to be that much slower. The fewer growing points to the bulb the shorter will be the time it will take the bulb to recover from its period in the pot. Rate of recovery does depend to some extent upon the natural vigour of the cultivar but after one season in a pot a bulb can often require two seasons in the open ground to return to its true size. Cultivars also vary in their ability to achieve bulbs of a particular size and this must be taken into account when determining if a bulb is large enough to give a good return from pot cultivation.

With modern developments and understanding of composts each grower has a number of options available but they can be broadly categorised as 'soil based' or 'no soil'. Each category has its advocates though currently the majority seem to favour soil-based compost, despite the fact that its greater density and water-retaining capability make pots that much heavier for moving around. The no-soil compost has a more reliable and reproducible quality, is less dense and therefore lighter to carry around, but demands much more critical attention to watering if the pots are not to dry out. Recent developments appear to have overcome the problem of no-soil composts encouraging the development of basal rot and similar diseases and such composts can be of assistance in producing ideal conditions for difficult cultivars such as Rainbow (2W-WWP), Grand Prospect (2Y-W) or Viking (1Y-Y).

My own preference is still for the soil-based compost based upon the John Innes formula. However, as something of a compromise and to reduce the density of the medium, I use perlite (expanded volcanic granules) to ensure adequate drainage through the compost yet retain a water-holding capability so that absorbable water is readily available at all times. The mix of the compost I use varies in distinct levels within each pot and there are further variations dependent upon the vigour previously experienced in blooms of each cultivar. For example, Empress of Ireland (1W-W) will be liberally treated with inorganic fertiliser to give size without too much risk of 'rots' whereas Camelot (2Y-Y) will be kept short of all fertilisers to reduce coarseness but will have an increase of perlite to hold water to retain size.

Before planting, all of my various composts and additives are collected together in the potting area so that they are readily accessible. My sequence then is to fill each pot in the order of the defined layers, as follows:

Layer 1 — about $1\frac{1}{2}$ to 2in (4 to 5cm) of a mix of 50 per cent standard John Innes No 3 and 50 per cent well-rotted organic manure. The two are thoroughly mixed together and gently firmed into the bottom of the pot.

Layer 2 — sufficient material to fill the pot to within 4 to 5in (10 to 12cm) of the rim (dependent upon the size of the bulbs). This is a mix of 85 per cent standard John Innes No 3 and 15 per cent perlite. As this effectively dilutes the fertiliser in the compost, additional inorganic balanced fertiliser is incorporated during the mixing and is preferably of a slow-releasing formulation. This is then well firmed to provide a base for the placement of the bulbs.

Layer 3 — a shallow layer of well-washed gravel, either $\frac{1}{8}$in (3mm) or $\frac{1}{4}$in (6mm), to ensure good drainage immediately beneath the bulbs.

Layer 4 — the bulbs are stood upright on the layer of gravel and always around the edge of the pot to keep the centre clear for subsequent staking, then good sterilised garden soil or John Innes No 3 is added to fill all the gaps around and between the bulbs. This layer, after being compressed, should ideally be $\frac{1}{2}$ to 1in (1 to 2cm) below the rim of the pot but must be level with the tips of the bulbs.

Layer 5 — washed gravel is added to fill the pot to its rim. This will be tipped out when the bulbs are ultimately lifted from their winter plunge bed, to leave a watering space at the top of the pot. The layer of gravel has a low friction effect so it can be removed without disturbing the underlying compost.

As each pot is filled in this sequence a suitable label is inserted down the side. I attach a plastic label to a small length of wood which then stands 4 to 5in (10 to 12cm) above the surface to act as a guide to ensure that the pot is buried deeply enough in its winter quarters. The wood label support is also useful as an aid to gripping the pot for carrying. As potting progresses it is advisable to water an odd pot or two to check that the compost is not too firm to impede the free passage of water.

Most people will develop their own compost mixes based upon experience with other subjects or upon results from a previous daffodil season. Satisfactory results with a particular mix for other subjects are likely to transfer to daffodils — an understanding of your compost and its water-retaining ability is important. Experimentation with different compost mixes may help to identify one which you find easier to manage but until you have an idea of the outcome a wholesale change should not be made. Traditionally the 'crocking' of pots has been advocated not only to improve drainage but to impede worms etc in their search for comfortable quarters. I have never resorted to 'crocking' with plastic pots and have not had any adverse effects. However, if you believe in 'crocking' then do it in combination with your preferred compost mix.

Winter quarters for the pots are important and are usually referred to as a plunge bed. The basic requirement is for an area which is large enough for the pots to be stood in a single layer though they can be packed against one another. A trench can be dug under a wall or hedge but there must be good drainage; sloping ground is easier or alternatively a good layer of coarse gravel should be used to form a base. If there is some form of retaining structure the pots can be stood on the ground, though if such a framework is of brick or stone a severe frost may penetrate and damage the bulbs. Whichever approach is adopted, any gaps between the pots need filling with soil, peat or some similar material and then a 4 to 5in (10 to 12cm) protective layer should cover the surfaces of the pots. Ideally the covering material should be free of anything which may impede the free passage of the growth as it emerges from the bulbs. It is possible to use straw or bracken but it must be held in place.

If you are sufficiently organised at planting time it may be possible to group the pots so that the early-flowering cultivars are at one end of the plunge bed and there is gradual progression through to the later-flowering cultivars at the opposite end — this may help to get pots out in a suitable sequence for timing the blooms. If severe frosts can be expected at lifting time it may be appro-priate to use a supplementary layer of straw, or equivalent, as an insulation material so that the pots can be lifted without the risk of damage through attempts to remove frozen compost from their surfaces. Alternatively, the pots can be covered with pine needles, which do not freeze into a solid mass.

Availability of bulbs from the selected cultivars will dictate just how soon the planting and plunging can be completed. The aim should be to have it all done as soon as possible after bulbs have been lifted and treated to give them the maximum time in which to produce their root system. This usually means late summer, which often coincides with a period of dry weather. Once the filled pots are in the plunge bed they should be kept well moistened by water-ing or by rainfall so that growth is initiated properly and is continuous. If the plunge bed is located under a wall or hedge it may not receive the full benefit of the autumn rains and if it appears at all dry it should be watered.

Throughout the following weeks the surface of the plunge bed should be checked over and any fallen leaves or debris which might impede the development of the shoots must be removed. Also, any hollows created by shrinkage of the covering material into the gaps between the pots should be filled to give good insulation from potential frost damage. As the days begin to lengthen some of the earlier-flowering cultivars may have their shoots visible; these can be attractive to slugs and snails and as a precautionary measure an early application of 'Noble' is advisable as this will penetrate to a sufficient depth to kill those pests in hiding between the pots. An alternative is a surface sprinkling of slug pellets or bait with suitable precautions to pro-tect pets or wildlife.

In early spring, about eight or nine weeks before the major shows, the pots should be removed from the plunge bed. The timing will depend upon many variables and some of the later-flowering cultivars may need extra early lift-ing. Care should be taken to avoid damage to the pots and more especially to

IN EARLY SPRING, pots of exhibition bulbs need moving from their winter quarters (the plunge bed) into the protection of a cold greenhouse. The 4in (10cm) layer of covering material needs removing so that the shoots, label and pot can be well cleaned to make for ease of handling later

the shoots which may be quite tiny or up to some 5 to 6in (12 to 15cm) long. If there is a soil covering to the plunge, each pot as it is lifted can be laid on its side so that the plunge material falls away taking with it the layer of gravel used to fill the pot to its rim. At this stage it is advisable to try and get the pots dried so that they can be wiped free of loose dirt — better to do it at this stage than find that when blooms are being cut dirt is transferred to a choice flower because hands have become soiled when moving pots.

The cleaned pots are then taken into the glasshouse for protection. They may be stood on the floor or on staging as preferred. I prefer to have my pots on the floor so that when the blooms are developed they are at a convenient height for examination: a further advantage is that the cooler air nearer the ground is beneficial for bloom development and can be kept that much more humid. Pots on staging are more convenient for access for watering/feeding and for tying up of blooms but the flowers are that much closer to the glass and more likely to be affected by changes of light and temperature. Whichever approach is adopted, consideration needs to be given to protection of the young shoots that have been deprived of the covering of plunge material. The tips of the shoots may be damaged if they are exposed to bright sunlight early in the day and a protective layer of paper, until they have turned green, is advantageous — some advocate newspaper, some tissue paper. One or two growers favour protecting all growth that is not green and will tie paper collars around each shoot. With pots standing on the ground, and good natural shade early in the day, this is not really necessary.

83

From this time onwards it is important to ensure that the conditions in the greenhouse are such that the compost in the pots is not allowed to freeze. It is also important to provide full and good ventilation so that the environment is cool enough to prevent the developing shoots becoming drawn. This usually means that all windows and doors must be kept open on any day when the ambient temperature rises above 32°F (0°C), though they must be closed overnight. If overnight heating is provided it needs very careful management so that it is just sufficient to keep the air temperature at 34°F, or at most 36°F (1° to 2°C).

For the first two weeks or so the pots should not require a lot of attention. However, preparations must be made for subsequent watering and as blooms start to develop large quantities of water will be required each day. A hose-pipe connected direct to the mains makes the task much lighter but the spray of water must not be strong enough to wash compost from the pots. This method allows aerated water to be drawn into the compost and, with the modern attachments, liquid fertilisers can easily be applied as frequently as necessary. Rainwater, collected in tubs or butts, may be chemically advantageous, particularly in areas where the main water supply is fluoridised, but the still water may not give the same aeration to the compost.

The commencement of feeding the pots becomes a matter for assessment related to the amount of water that has passed through each pot and taken away the soluble chemicals that provide the food. I usually start applying liquid fertilisers, high in potash content but with a proportion of nitrogen and phosphate, say, 'Chempak', 'Phostrogen' or proprietary tomato feed, about four weeks before the dates of the major shows. Low concentrations are used, about 20 per cent of manufacturer's recommendation, but the liquid feed is applied at each watering except where conditions are such that pots require watering two, three or more times per day. This liquid fertiliser is applied right up to the time the pots are removed from the greenhouse because the blooms have finished.

As development of the shoots progresses foliage and flower stems will need support. A 24in (60cm) split cane can be inserted into the centre of each pot with a length of soft twine attached and passed in a series of loops around the foliage from each bulb. These loops can gradually be raised up the cane as growth develops — one set of ties is usually sufficient for any cultivar. As stems elongate they have a tendency to bend towards the direction of greatest light intensity and to help maintain erect, strong stems pots should be rotated through 90 degrees at least once a day. This rotation needs to be carefully assessed as the buds begin to break and the neck bends, and blooms must not be allowed to come into contact with one another.

As blooms begin to develop assessments will have to be made to ensure that they are going to be ready for the appointed show day. It usually takes ten days from bud break to achievement of full potential but this time will be drastically reduced if temperatures soar to the 80°F (27°C) range or extended if the temperatures fall to below 45°F (7°C). Shading of the greenhouse may be essential if days are bright and sunny and for preference this should be done with one of the plastic netting materials which can be removed readily on dull sunless days. Skill at forecasting daily conditions will have to be acquired or otherwise some arrangement made for changing the shading and ventilation. It may be advisable to have one area of the greenhouse with some very dense shading, say cotton sheeting, where those cultivars that have red cups can be allowed to develop without any risk of burning of the rim of the corona or fading of the intensity of the colouring. Additionally, shading means that the air within the greenhouse, with all the ventilation open, will be damper and thereby encourage the blooms to develop substance.

Spraying of the atmosphere two or three times per day will naturally help to maintain humidity, as will watering the ground around the pots. However, there are certain risks with these methods: large drops of water accumulating on a part of the flower will act as a focusing lens and can cause spotting of the bloom; also, though the aim is to keep the pots and ground well moistened so that the bulbs can take up ample water for the developing bloom, the environment may become so stale and damp that the necks of the bulbs begin to rot. Electric fans are most useful for ensuring that air does not become stagnant. During this period of bloom development it may also be necessary to avoid very low temperatures. This implies some form of heating that will be triggered into operation when the temperatures fall below 36°F (2°C) and electric fan type equipment is ideal as it gives air movement even if most of the ventilators have been closed for the night.

If blooms are developing too rapidly a change of environment can retard growth. This usually means moving the relevant pot into a cool room where stability of temperature is essential. The cooler the temperature the slower will be the development of the bloom. It is also beneficial to have a low light intensity. In some cases it may be sufficient simply to stand the pot outside the greenhouse, provided it is protected from the wind. Even with only one cultivar to a pot the blooms will not all be at identical stages of development and if one is significantly more advanced the best answer may be to cut it and stand it in clean water in a darkened and cool room, leaving the others to develop in the pot and catch up.

Blooms that are not developing quickly enough for the intended show date may need some encouragement. This necessitates careful manipulation of light and heat to simulate ideal growing conditions. Heat on its own will encourage growth but there is the risk that it will produce drawn stems and foliage and a weakened flower. Light on its own will also encourage growth but without loss of substance of the bloom. The two in combination can produce relatively normal growth and allow the bloom to achieve substance and size. A separate area must be used for this activity and needs to have heating which can be thermostatically controlled, air that is moved with a fan, and suitable lighting. Fluorescent tubing gives an appropriate spectrum of lighting. It needs to be arranged in such a way that it can be adjusted, at least daily, to keep the tubes about 6 to 8in (15 to 20cm) above the growing tips of the leaves. It is the intensity of light at the growing tips which determines the rate of development. The pots need to be kept moist at all times with a weak solution of liquid fertiliser and benefits can be gained by standing the pots in suitable plastic saucers which can hold a shallow depth of fertiliser solution — this also helps to give a damp atmosphere and water at the roots.

A wide range of standard cultivars respond very well to this combination of heat and light provided that the temperature is maintained at 55°F (13°C) as a minimum and the lights are on for twelve or thirteen hours per day. A period of darkness each day maintains the natural cycle and allows the plant to consolidate growth. Merlin (3W-YYR), Passionale (2W-P), Daydream (2Y-W) and similar cultivars will develop from a height of 6in (15cm) to fully-developed blooms in approximately twenty-one days. Some of the miniature cultivars also respond very well and good results have been achieved with Hawera (5Y-Y), Pencrebar (4Y-Y) and Clare (7Y-Y). Yellow perianth cultivars can give good results as long as the temperatures are not too high. Red-cupped cultivars do respond reasonably well and the light intensity from a pair of fluorescent tubes is usually sufficient to encourage growth without causing burning of the corona. Some cultivars are not suited to this manipulation and whilst they may produce reasonably acceptable blooms to complete a collection they suffer serious deterioration of the bulbs.

POTS FOR EFFECT

The basic system is almost identical to the arrangements adopted to produce cut blooms. However, the main aim is to produce the maximum impact from a given size of pot with all blooms as near to full development as possible for the designated day.

Unless the show schedule specifies both the size of the pot and the number of bulbs, the aim should be to pack as many bulbs as possible in a pot. The ability of bulbs to produce flowers at the same height even though the planting depths are different enables two layers of bulbs to be planted, thereby increasing the number of blooms to a given size of pot. Again, one cultivar to a pot is essential to give an evenness of height and a uniform appearance.

To ensure an all-round effect of blooms as well as encouraging upright growth the pots should be rotated through 90 degrees at least once a day. Tying up of the foliage needs to be done in such a way as to be unobtrusive, the system of looping twine around the foliage from each bulb and back to a central cane is very effective. Short-growing cultivars are preferable so that any hastening of development with heat still does not produce a mass of blooms that appears top heavy.

CUT BLOOMS FROM THE GARDEN

Most cultivars respond very well when grown in the garden. However, if exhibition blooms are required there are a number of points which need to be taken into account:

- Bulbs usually produce their best-quality blooms the second season after planting.
- Competition with other subjects can reduce the potential of a particular cultivar.
- Protection will need to be provided to eliminate damage to the developing blooms. It must be removed after flowering to give the foliage as natural a growth pattern as possible.
- Some system may have to be devised for watering without the risk of splashing or marking the developing blooms.

It is usual to plant exhibition cultivars in a separate area which has been well manured for a previous crop. If space does not permit such a rotation of cropping, daffodils can be grown on the same ground for many years but periodic sterilisation of the soil will be necessary and beneficial. Recognising that you will need to get to all parts of the bed to examine blooms and cut them without risk of damage to other blooms or foliage a maximum width of 4ft (125cm) is realistic. The traditional practice of parallel beds separated by the same width of pathway uses a lot of space and narrower paths are acceptable. In real terms most growers will space out their ground to match the area that needs protection.

Not everyone has ground that is ideally suited to daffodils and some system of raised beds is usually adopted. This means that soil from the pathways will be added to the top of the defined planting area. In confined spaces the raising of the bed is still essential and it may be necessary to use edging boards to define the limits of the bed and increase the practical width to be used for planting. Raising of the surface of the beds by 4in (10cm) will ensure a significant improvement in the drainage under the bulbs and eliminate the risk of development of rots.

To assist in locating bulbs and to avoid the risk of cultivars becoming mixed at lifting time it is prudent to plant the bulbs in straight rows across the bed. It is also helpful to produce a planting plan which clearly locates each cultivar and also records the number of bulbs of each which have been

RAISED BEDS have been created with edgings of substantial timbers to maximise planting space. Planting is undertaken from a board to reduce compaction of the soil. Off-sets and double-nosed bulbs are alternated along the row to encourage evenness of growth. Stout labels need to be inserted as work proceeds. As the bulbs are covered the next trench is dug ready for another row

AN EFFICIENT ARRANGEMENT of protection for exhibition blooms. The whole plot has a netting wind-break and the central bed has been edged with corrugated acrylic sheeting fixed to stout wooden frames. The structure is substantial enough to carry top sheeting for advancing growth. At this stage, green, woven nylon netting can be rolled out over the frame to protect coloured coronas from the sun

planted. There are all sorts of possible planting sequences and one suitable to your own requirements must be developed. My preference is to group cultivars of the same Division together but trying to avoid similar-coloured cultivars being planted adjacent to one another. Thus, when cutting for a collection I can readily assess what is available from each Division and there is little chance of confusing blooms from two different cultivars. Other growers prefer to plant so that all cultivars flowering at the same time are kept together and protection can be readily installed at the correct time for the whole batch.

It is helpful if all bulbs likely to produce blooms suitable for exhibition can be planted in the prepared area. Surplus bulbs and those of insufficient size should be planted in a separate area to avoid cluttering up space that is to be given the necessary protection. Planting should proceed as early as practicable and no special attention is then necessary until growth is well established in the following spring. The greater the space that can be allowed between the bulbs the better, as this reduces the risk of blooms being damaged by accidental contact during growth; it also allows greater opportunity for staking blooms at flowering without risk of damage to the bulbs. Ideally, a minimum of 6in (15cm) should be allowed along a row and 12in (30cm) between rows. Such spacing also makes it easier to keep the soil surface clear of competing weeds once the daffodil foliage is well developed.

Some system of rotational planting is worthy of consideration, bearing in mind that better flowers can be expected the second season after planting. Once a reasonable number of bulbs of a particular cultivar have been accumulated they should be divided into two batches and planted in separate areas. Thus, one batch can be lifted the first year and the other the second year to establish a cycle allowing annual lifting of each cultivar and the benefit of blooms from bulbs that have been undisturbed for two seasons.

The practice of erecting a protective structure around the developing flowers is well established and has been used in various ways for well over fifty years. The developments in plastics and acrylics complement the traditional materials such as hessian and calico. The opportunities are virtually unlimited and are only dependent upon the ingenuity of the grower and the amount of money that is available. Systems can protect a defined area or an individual bloom or any particular combinations. Commercially available 'polytunnels' need their formal frames assembled at the time of planting to ensure that the bulbs are within the defined area, with due allowances for the curvature of the sides. Such tunnels are useful but they do not give good air circulation and they are not too easily managed where shading is required to protect cultivars from burning. Other systems have their advantages and disadvantages but whichever one is adopted it needs to:

●provide top covering to protect from rain, hail, snow etc which would otherwise damage the flowers;

- provide side covering to prevent wind damage;
- give a ready facility for shading blooms from direct sunlight;
- allow easy access for cutting blooms;
- allow for watering with little risk of splashing blooms.

It is important to erect the structure at the right time, and this depends on its purpose.

To advance the flowering date: small cloches/frames will be needed about three months before the normal flowering date. They will have to be followed by other systems.

To assist in advancing the blooms either marginally or significantly: large frames must be erected about one month before normal flowering date. If significantly earlier blooms are required some form of electric lighting may be necessary and if normal tungsten filament bulbs are used there will be some gain of heat as well as of light.

To protect the opening blooms with little alteration to their normal flowering dates: large structures that support shading or sheeting should be erected near to normal flowering date.

If protection is given too early there is a risk that stems will become drawn and the flowers thinned. Left in place for too long, there will be a premature collapse of foliage with detrimental effects on the bulbs.

Whatever is adopted as the major system of protection will probably not suit the requirements of each cultivar. Ancillary systems will be needed to give high-density localised shading, localised extra lighting or extra humidity. Once protection is in place it must be checked regularly to ensure that it has not moved or that stems have not elongated exceptionally so that opening blooms risk damage from contact with the structure. Also periodic examination must be made to make sure that the protected environment for the blooms has not become a luxury home for insect pests and in particular slugs.

Temperature records and some noting of sunlight, rain etc are invaluable aids when the grower is attempting to assess the season by comparison with previous years. Some attention must also be given to the condition of the ground, especially with regard to watering in lieu of rain and to the need for fertilising. The overall aim must be to try and provide the best possible conditions for the flowers, the foliage and the bulbs.

It is helpful if records can be maintained of the blooms used from under the protection on different dates. This will, over a period of years, identify those cultivars which respond well to certain systems and which ones are not compatible with your own regime. Coupled with the record of the seasonal characteristics, projections can then be made of what improvements are needed and which cultivars to persevere with for early, mid-season and late shows.

•6•
Showing Daffodils

A show is never likely to be a collection of perfect blooms. Each grower will try to assemble the best blooms available on the day; most of them will be good examples of the particular cultivars but will have been presented in such a way that they appear to visitors to be approaching the ultimate standard of perfection. In addition to giving the opportunity to see the modern introductions, shows also give many chances of learning more about the cultivation of the genus. Most exhibitors have their own views, theories and practices of cultivation and of the potentials of the different cultivars, and are prepared to talk about them and listen to other points of view — an interesting way of learning.

A GOOD BLOOM

A good bloom is not easily defined. What may be regarded as a good cultivar or bloom for garden display or floral art may not match the modern requirements for show purposes even though it can produce the occasional success. Perfection of detail, or absence of faults, is a simple starting point; however, if the characteristics of all the Divisions are to be allowed for then the good bloom needs a more complex definition. Using basic principles that have general application, the features and characteristics of a daffodil can be identified and assessed. (A number of accepted points systems are reproduced as Appendix II.) Form and poise, condition and texture, colour, size and stem all need to be right and in balance for the style of the particular cultivar.

The main requirement is 'form', a balance and roundness based upon a circular outline and a symmetry of the two halves of the flower — each effectively being a perfect mirror image of the other. Balance is not dependent upon the shape or size of the perianth segments, which may be circular, pointed or spade shaped, nor upon the style of the corona, but is concerned with the distribution of the essential parts around the central point of the flower, the stigma. In most cases the tips of the perianth segments will be spaced equidistantly around the circumference of the imaginary circle which forms the outline of the bloom. Indeed, the perianth is really two layers of segments, the tips of each layer being at the tips of two equilateral triangles, each possibly having slightly different dimensions. Symmetry and roundness

91

EXHIBITION BLOOMS need to be both round and symmetrical to create a nicely balanced effect. (Top left) The tips of the six perianth segments form a perfect circle but the shape and size varies so that the bloom lacks symmetry either side of a vertical line through the centre; (top right) the bloom is far from round, but left and right-hand halves of the flower are perfect mirror images of each other; (centre) the bloom is both round and symmetrical either side of a central line through the flower. Symmetry will be assessed by the judges at the back of the bloom as well as the front. (Bottom left) A nice round outline but unbalanced to the left and right of the central axis; (bottom right) a nice round outline with a symmetrical arrangement of the perianth segments

are closely interrelated, one without the other resulting in a bloom that is clearly not perfect.

The shape of the perianth segments is not the same in every cultivar though they have individual characteristics to make each cultivar distinctive. Allowances must be made for these differences and yet the concept of symmetry must be retained. With the double daffodils (Division 4) there still needs to be roundness of outline created by the outer six perianth segments and symmetry in the arrangement of the petaloids to give an overall balance to the bloom. Styles of bloom have changed over the years, so that the modern cultivars have very broad perianth segments which are well over-lapped for the greater part of their length, and this enhances the impression of roundness, but still there is the need to retain the symmetry. A good bloom should have the same degree of symmetry when viewed from behind — indeed this is the real starting point for the assessment of a bloom.

The coronas of daffodils can have many different shapes and styles and irrespective of these differences must have roundness and symmetry to main-tain balance. There is no clearly defined number of areas or sections to the corona, especially where it whorls or is frilled, but each must be equally spaced around the edge if it is to look correct.

As well as having the degree of balanced roundness described above, the good bloom will have good poise and will be well held at the end of the stem.

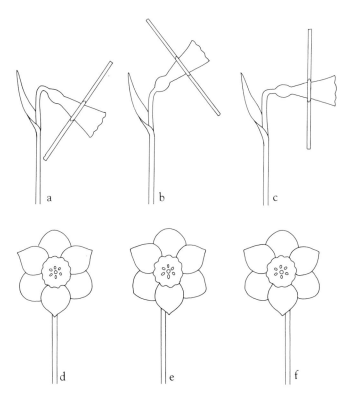

THE POISE OF A BLOOM is important and should be assessed from the side and front: (a) except for cyclamineus or triandus hybrids a hanging head is regarded as a serious fault; (b) a bloom that faces upwards will always be penalised for its poise; (c) the correct poise for all except cyclamineus and triandus hybrids and some of the species; (d) the neck is holding the bloom at the correct angle; (e) the bloom is held too far to the right, and (f) the bloom is held to the left, both examples of poor poise

The neck should have a shape and strength to hold the bloom at right angles to the stem when viewed from the side and in a vertical line when viewed from the front. Some cultivars have particularly weak necks and rarely hold the blooms correctly yet they still win prizes because of their perfection in the other areas; examples are Altruist (3O-R), Silver Leopard (3W-WWY) or Acropolis (4W-R).

Poise with some of the blooms from the minor Divisions is difficult to assess and blooms or florets held precisely at right angles would be faulted. The cyclamineus types (Division 6) must retain the characteristic hanging of the head to be of correct form. The triandus hybrids (Division 5) must be gracefully nodding and therefore suitable allowances are made. Multi-headed cultivars should hold the individual florets so that they can be seen as individuals within a compact whole. Poor poise allows the florets to droop and creates unsightly gaps in the total bloom.

Looking beyond the basic requirements and continuing the quest for perfection, a good daffodil should be free of nicks, tears, creases or signs of physical damage, especially around the edge of each perianth segment and the corona. There is no distinction drawn between naturally occurring faults or those which have been caused accidentally. The edges of the perianth segments can be so easily damaged and each mark will be penalised. These are criticisms of the condition of the bloom and there are other related issues. Signs of ageing should not be visible, especially any browning of the tips of the perianth segments, dull greyish colouring of the pollen on the stamens or collapse of the edges of the perianth segments or the corona. A good bloom will have a firm, rigid perianth and corona and no signs of any part beginning to go transparent.

The substance and size of the bloom must be appropriate to the cultivar. Some cultivars, for example Golden Aura (2Y-Y) and Loch Stac (2Y-R), more nearly approach perfection of condition and form when they are under their typical size so it is a case of trying to assess the merits of the whole bloom. Other cultivars, such as Arkle (1Y-Y), Camelot (2Y-Y) or Empress of Ireland (1W-W), are capable of producing blooms of great size and whilst they may retain their characteristic and satisfactory form they tend to have a coarseness of texture not appropriate to an exhibition bloom. Size for the sake of size is not a benefit but has to be assessed as a part of the whole.

In all cases the colour, typical of the cultivar, must be pure and clear: fading, streaking or muddiness are not appropriate or acceptable. Some cultivars display slight variations of colour distribution depending upon growing conditions and generally this is not regarded as a fault unless it really departs from the registration details. Various discussions take place on the question of 'staining' (colour from the corona running onto the perianth segments) or 'flushing' (corona colour suffusing the perianth segments to create the impression of a new colour combination) and these are never conclusive. In general terms, 'flushing' is acceptable whilst 'staining' is not. Patchiness of colour is really frowned upon and indeed some of the worst cases of patchiness are the results of either virus infection of the bulb or sun scorch through the magnification effects of water droplets on the bloom. It is also recognised that some cultivars develop or change their colouring as the blooms develop through to maturity but in all cases the colouring must be pure and relate to the registration details. However, the reverse bicolours often take some time to attain their correct whiteness of corona and in a class for this type would be penalised if exhibited before the true colouring had emerged. Red and orange colouring in the corona unfortunately burns quite readily in bright sunlight and where this has occurred it will invariably be regarded as a serious fault. Where the corona is rimmed and displays a number of hues then uneven distribution or fading of the colouring can give the impression that the bloom is less than perfect. In other respects the colouring of the cultivar, including any staining or flushing which is characteristic, would rarely be penalised.

With the multi-headed cultivars size and substance are important but of greater concern is the number of florets and their arrangement. There must be sufficient florets to be typical of the cultivar against a notional norm as assessed over many years. A reduction in the number gives each floret more room to develop and this usually reduces creasing and other damage to the perianth segments. The number of florets does not override considerations of shape and evenness of size but is taken into account; for example, a bloom of Highfield Beauty (8Y-GYO) with two perfectly round, symmetrical and even-sized florets will usually fare better than a bloom of the same cultivar with three round, unsymmetrical and different-sized florets. Faults in the perianths are less obvious if the individual florets are not fully developed or are still buds and thus to avoid a penalty any multi-headed stem should be shown when at least 50 per cent of the florets are fully developed. Some cultivars, such as Avalanche (8W-Y), have a very large number of florets and careful removal of one or two that are damaged or showing signs of ageing may be beneficial and not result in a penalty or detract from the overall beauty.

Miniature cultivars are difficult to assess to the same standards of perfection though they should have the basics of a good bloom. By definition they should have a gracefulness of form appropriate to their size. Roundness of outline is desirable, though with some species, such as the bulbocodiums and N cyclamineus, it may be difficult to detect roundness other than in the rim of the corona. Most classes for miniatures require three blooms per vase and therefore the objective should be to utilise blooms displaying the greatest similarity in all factors.

THE SHOW SCHEDULE

In an ideal situation an intending exhibitor will visit a particular show one year to assess what is going to be required of him in the next. This is not always possible and so other sources of information have to be used — fortunately, most show secretaries will willingly give advice about facilities, vases etc. Naturally the published schedule for the show will be an invaluable help in addition to spelling out the composition of each exhibit.

Likely exhibits should be preplanned so that the right number of blooms from the appropriate Divisions are gathered together or identified in advance. Show schedules tend to use standardised descriptions which assume some degree of familiarity with what is expected, for example: twelve cultivars, one stem of each, from not less than four Divisions staged one bloom per vase. Such a definition makes no reference to the colour of the blooms but by convention there should be an equal number of blooms with yellow perianths and with white perianths. There is nothing to prevent all having white perianths or all having yellow perianths but this may result in some loss of points for the overall exhibit in tight competition. Equally, there is nothing to restrict the choice of the required four Divisions but an exhibitor who selects from Divisions 1, 2, 3 and 4 is choosing cultivars which are more likely to produce blooms nearer to perfection and more likely, because of their size similarity, to make a better-balanced exhibit. Division 9 is a useful alternative to Division 4, but the use of Division 11 is likely to expose prejudices against the split coronas. Cultivars from Division 6 with the characteristic drooping head will disturb the balance of the exhibit as will multi-headed cultivars from Divisions 5, 7 or 8. There is no requirement to have a defined number of cultivars from each of the four selected Divisions so long as there is at least one from each; however, if two exhibits were equal in all other respects then a balance across the Divisions would be likely to tilt the decision.

Some schedules include price limit classes and these demand careful attention. Where reference is made to a published listing, for example that maintained by the Daffodil Society, only those cultivars included in the list are eligible for showing in the classes — the use of any others or of unnamed seedlings will result in disqualification. Where no such listing is defined, careful records must be maintained so that evidence is available if the eligibility of a particular cultivar is challenged.

With the increased attention to miniatures more classes are now being provided in local and national shows. Two basic systems are adopted to determine eligibility of cultivars to be shown as miniatures and the exhibit must conform to the defined requirements. If the class calls for entries selected from the list of approved miniatures adopted by the Daffodil Society and the American Daffodil Society, then a quality bloom of a recognised cultivar is always acceptable even if the cultivation has produced a little extra size. The alternative system, whereby entries must comply with the size limit defined by the Royal Horticultural Society, gives the exhibitor a wider range of cultivars as potential exhibits but each bloom will have to be checked when being cut, and again just before judging to ensure that it has not developed in water, or since being staged, and exceeded the defined size.

Careful study of the schedule is essential. It can help in planning ahead for what to grow for particular classes but, more importantly, it can ensure that preselection of blooms is undertaken prior to cutting so that adequate blooms are available to fulfil any entries which are submitted in advance.

CUTTING FOR THE SHOW

As each bloom begins to open it is possible to start assessing its potential for the show-bench. Great care must be taken to avoid damaging the young flower or bending its neck too far to get a better view — this can result in the total destruction of the bloom by breaking it from the stem and cause much frustration and anger.

A study of the back view of the young flower will give a ready initial assessment of its likely ultimate roundness and symmetry as well as enabling the edge of each petal to be examined for critical nicks or tears. Once it is established that the bloom has some potential it should be examined from the front for symmetry of outline and absence of damage which may have been caused where a petal has become entangled with the developing corona. The edge of the corona needs to be examined, too, for tears or major damage or for lack of balance. A corona of Division 1 or 2 cultivars may be complete but lacking in a degree of roundness; this should not cause rejection of the bloom as some manipulation during staging (see page 102) may improve its appearance.

Although the spathe will not really be considered during the judging of the bloom it must be in place. If it has been a particularly strong bud the withering spathe may rub and damage a perianth segment or even pierce it. If such damage is thought likely, some manipulation may be needed at this stage. The spathe on a multi-headed cultivar may also need easing away from the necks of the florets to give each one room to develop. It may also be worth considering if any additional support should be provided to hold each stem vertically and to prevent two or more blooms rubbing against each other.

A false impression of roundness can be created if the bloom under consideration has more than six perianth segments or if there are five over-sized ones. This variation from the norm should be checked as any deviation will result in disqualification. Variations from the norm of six perianth segments are particularly prevalent amongst the multi-headed cultivars and so each floret which appears as part of the bloom needs to be checked most carefully, but in all other respects the roundness and symmetry of each floret must be judged as for a single-headed cultivar.

Other factors may need to be considered dependent upon the level of competition which can be anticipated. For instance, the grower may try to forecast the ultimate size of the bloom for matching into a multi-bloom exhibit. Clarity of colour may be important, particularly of reversed bicolours or where there is a risk of the colour being burnt out of the bloom by too much exposure to sunlight. The cutting must not be left to chance but done with some semblance of order and without too much of a last-minute panic.

Once the good blooms that meet the requirements of the schedule have been selected an entry can be made and steps taken to get the blooms to the show-bench in the best condition possible. It is always preferable to cut a bloom at least forty-eight hours before the show. My own method is to make a clean cut with a very sharp blade at right angles to the stem at a point where it is fully green; other exhibitors prefer an oblique cut or to snap the stem, but the damage to stem cells must be minimised if they are to be able to take up water for the flower. The stem should be placed into water as quickly as possible, and before too much sap is exuded, and this will help to ensure that some development of the bloom will take place even after it has been cut. Some exhibitors advocate the immediate plunging of stems into deep water, others advocate plunging into only 2 or 3in (5 or 7cm) of warm water with subsequent transfer to deep water after the temperature has fallen naturally to the ambient. Whichever approach is adopted the stem must be kept in a condition to absorb water for the developing bloom.

The degree of development after cutting will depend upon the storage temperature and the light intensity — low temperatures and darkness will virtually hold the bloom in its current state. It is possible to store blooms in a refrigerator provided the temperature is reliably set at 36°F (2.2°C), but the ends of the stems need to be immersed in shallow water or well moistened moss and the blooms should not be in contact with abrasive surfaces. The technique needs trial with the facilities available but blooms can be held in reasonable condition for about fourteen days and will survive for a number of days on the show-bench if the correct conditions have been maintained. However, the late developer or the one prone to sun scorch may need warmth and some light to bring it to the required development for showing. Some cultivars, such as Altruist (3O-R) and Kimmeridge (3W-YYO), are better cut in the bud stage and allowed to develop slowly over five or six days in subdued lighting to avoid any scorch damage to the rim of the corona. Where blooms are stored in water the end of each stem needs to be checked at least once a day for splitting or curling — sure signs that water is not being taken up — and as necessary fresh clean cuts should be made above the split or curling. Generally, after twenty-four hours in water the blooms can be packed for transportation either dry or in a smaller quantity of water.

During the period of storage and conditioning it is also possible to be doing some work that will ease the load at the show hall. As each bloom is going to be handled and looked at a number of times the opportunity can be taken to do some of the basic grooming, such as removal of dirt splashes and dust, and some manipulation of the perianth. Also, where sufficient space is available, each possible exhibit can be gathered together and adjusted as additional blooms are cut, which will enable the blooms to be packed in logical sequences or indeed the best set and spares to be put into containers ready for the journey.

TRANSPORT TO THE SHOW

For long journeys dry-packing is safest, provided the blooms can be held rigidly in place to eliminate friction damage from the container, packing material or neighbouring blooms. Some exhibitors suggest tight packing of the blooms so that they cushion one another but I try to keep each bloom separate and protected by soft paper and held in place by tapes. My boxes are made of wood and are sometimes difficult to handle although they do have advantages and can double as additional staging space. A roll of soft paper is laid across one end of the box and the first blooms are rested in position, avoiding contact with the sides of the box and other blooms. A further roll of soft paper is then gently wedged under the bottom half of the row of blooms so that it also doubles as the pillow for the next row. Once both ends of the box have been filled two rows of cotton tape are pinned across the centre to apply pressure to the stems and hold them in place.

PART OF A MULTI-VASE EXHIBIT packed dry for transporting to a show. The individual blooms are held safely in position between rolls of soft paper. Cotton tapes have been pinned across the centre of the box to keep the stems secure during the journey

Surplus cardboard boxes from the florist can often make suitable alternatives, though some system of holding the blooms in position needs to be improvised. Other systems and practices can be devised using plastics, foam rubber or anything sufficient to withstand the anticipated knocks and jolts in transit.

For local shows, and transporting multi-headed cultivars, I prefer to travel the stems in water, pre-staged in vases or packed into vases or bottles held in a suitable framework so that movement does not bring blooms into contact with one another. Transporting blooms in water certainly saves time at the show hall but correct packing is very time-consuming and more risky than dry-packing. Whichever method is adopted it is essential to retain as long a stem as possible to give greater scope when staging.

Although we all like to think we can identify the cultivars we have cut, the panic of staging can cause embarrassing memory lapses, so it is advisable to label each bloom by either a small tie-on price label or the simple expedient of a ball-point pen message low down on the dry stem.

Most exhibitors will want to take some spare blooms with them just in case there are casualties on the journey. Space and time available will give some guidance on how many extra blooms to pack. Too many spare blooms can be as bad as insufficient, particularly as they will all need handling at the show venue and may never get exhibited for lack of time or patience.

Good staging can be very time-consuming, especially where multi-vase exhibits are concerned, and due allowances must be made for possible problems on the journey. The route should be planned to avoid busy town centres with their inevitable stop/start performances and consequential risks of jolting the blooms. Motorways are monotonous and perhaps in mileage terms the longer routes but they are less likely to cause problems for the blooms. If travel in the middle of the day is inevitable it may be necessary to shade some of the car windows to help keep the temperature down and, where blooms are being travelled in water, to eliminate the risk of scorch damage to red-cupped cultivars.

STAGING THE FLOWERS

The art of staging needs much practice if the individual blooms or collections of blooms are going to be done full justice after the work that has so far gone into their production.

The exhibitor will need quite a collection of bits and pieces that will be pressed into service for staging purposes in addition to vases which are usually provided at the show hall and as detailed in the schedule. The most important ones are packing material for holding the blooms in the vases and a supply of leaves, cut from less expensive cultivars. Moss, that has been picked over to remove twigs, leaves etc, is the ideal packing material as it retains its natural springiness to hold the stems in their appointed positions and still permits water to flow freely. Even if an abundant supply is not available and alternative materials are used, a layer of moss on the top of the vase will enhance the appearance of the exhibit. Any leaves should be fresh and clean and of sizes appropriate to the cultivars to be staged.

Other bits will probably include a supply of cards for labelling the exhibits, provision pins (spring wire clips as used by the butcher for pricing his joints) for holding the labels in the vases, a towel for cleaning vases and drying hands before manipulating the blooms, brushes of different sizes and types for dressing the blooms or sweeping pollen from the corona, scissors for trimming the moss level with the top of the vase and sharp blades for trimming stems. (Each exhibitor will extend this list, according to experience, into such things as food, warm sweaters, etc, and it makes sense to pack everything into a special box well in advance of the journey to the show.)

On arrival at the appointed venue, find a place to work and after unloading the blooms and everything else move the car so that other exhibitors also have convenient access. Get blooms which have been travelled dry into buckets of slightly warmed water (which can be brought in vacuum flasks) and whilst they begin to recover collect your vases and prepare for staging. A surprisingly wide range of containers are pressed into service as vases for exhibition daffodils, but you must comply with any specified sizes or styles of vase dictated by the organisers and published in the show schedule. Small vases, such as the 7in (17cm) Bikini type (two plastic mouldings which when assembled give a tapered tube), are ideal for single blooms. Limit yourself to the number you will definitely need and not more than a couple of spares. Once you have got them to the table or area where you are to work, wipe them over to remove dust and dirt which has accumulated during storage. Fill them to within ¾in (2cm) of the rim with clean water and get organised for the placement of the blooms. Keep your supply of moss and leaves conveniently to hand on the staging table.

There must be a high degree of mathematical precision in the arrangement of an exhibit and a sensitive approach to colour combinations and balance. Single blooms are relatively straightforward, especially where being shown as individuals and height of staging is not critical. The bloom should be picked up and the leaves positioned along the back of the stem. The tips of the leaves should be about 1in (2.5cm) below the bottom edge of the perianth. The number of leaves will depend upon the number that can be sacrificed from garden cultivars or from pots specifically grown to give a supply of leaves. The width and size of the leaves should be in keeping with the type of bloom: broad leaves for Division 1 cultivars and narrow ones for Divisions 5 and 7. It is preferable to have three per stem, though a minimum of two is acceptable.

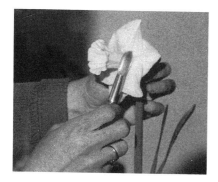

Dressing the blooms

A broad, soft, artist's paint brush can be rolled across each perianth segment to encourage it to stand at right angles to the neck of the flower and in a flat plane. Care must be exercised to avoid damage to the edges of the perianth, especially where there is a slight hooding at the tips. By careful repetition of this brushing movement it may be possible to remedy some slight creasing of the perianth segments, though it will never be eliminated. At this point a small soft brush, moistened with either clear water or saliva, can be used to remove dirt and dust from both front and back of the bloom — too much pressure can result in bruising or piercing of the surface which will be readily visible by the time of judging.

Attention should also be given to the corona, not only to ensure its cleanliness but to overcome any irregularity in its shaping. Manipulation is best done by using gentle pressure between thumb and fingers. Although the majority of cultivars will respond, particularly those from Divisions 1 and 2, too much movement may cause bruising, a fatal crack or a ripped edge.

Clocking of blooms is another refinement that can be attempted to improve appearance. This involves the rotation of the neck of the flower so that one of the perianth segments has its axis in line with the stem and its tip pointing vertically to the bench. Some cultivars, such as Camelot (2Y-Y), have short stiff necks and do not respond well to this treatment; there is a real risk that the neck will break so that you end up with flower in one hand and stem and vase in the other. It is a technique which requires careful practice on spare blooms at home if it is to be successful.

Adjusting the poise

At staging time it is possible to attempt to make some minor adjustments to the poise of the blooms. Slight variations of the positioning of the stem away from the vertical may be sufficient to get the flower looking straight ahead but the fault will still be evident to the judge. An alternative is to stage the flower and

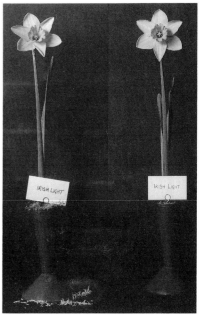

STAGING AND PRESENTATION do make a difference. The bloom on the left has been positioned in its vase without too much attention to detail. On the right is the same bloom looking altogether more impressive, having been restaged with additional leaves and set to a correct height, with the surface of the moss trimmed and debris removed. The bloom has been 'clocked', the perianth has been groomed to be at right angles to the neck, and the corona has been manipulated to a decent roundness

stand it facing a dark surface so that the greater intensity of light falling on its back will encourage it to lift to the more desirable angle — if this does happen the height of the flower may need adjustment to align with the rest of the exhibit.

Some cultivars, for example, Cool Crystal (3W-GWW), Tudor Minstrel (2W-Y) and Empress of Ireland (1W-W), hang their heads very badly, and it is worth trying to change the angle of poise by a more drastic approach prior to placing the bloom in its vase. The stem should be laid flat on the staging table, so that the bloom is facing to the floor just clear of the edge, and should be held in place with a good handful of wet moss over its cut end. A bloom left in this position for at least an hour, and preferably longer, will make some attempt to lift its head to the light and have a much better poise.

Final staging
For single-bloom entries all that is required is a neatly-written name-card located at the front of the vase and held in place by a provision pin. When carrying the vase to its appointed place, protect the flower from accidental damage and take care not to disturb other exhibits on the bench. Finally, check that the vase is clean and the stem upright, making any allowances for unevenness of the staging, and that the designated exhibitor card is placed with the exhibit.

STAGING THREE BLOOMS to a vase ideally requires three identical-sized examples of one cultivar, as in centre picture. With three different-sized blooms of one cultivar it is never possible to achieve a balanced effect and the slightly larger bloom is positioned at the top for preference, as on left. If two blooms are almost identical and the third is somewhat smaller a reasonably balanced effect can be obtained by arranging as on right

The tips of the leaves should be at slightly different heights, with the foremost two about 1in (2.5cm) lower than the back one. The ends of the stem and leaves should be trimmed off level with a sharp blade. The stem and leaves should be held in the vase so that they are 1in (2.5cm) clear of the base. Moss should then be packed all round the stem and pressed well down into the vase. The packing needs to be firm enough to hold the stem in a vertical position but not too tightly done to allow the stem and/or leaves to be raised or lowered without disturbing the moss. By placing the stem at the centre of the vase there will be some latitude to alter its angle from the vertical to display the bloom to its best advantage for viewing fully from the front. In collections of singly-staged blooms, all the blooms need precise alignment both horizontally and vertically and careful arrangement according to colour variations.

Three blooms of one cultivar in one vase need to be staged in a careful sequence at the corners of an equilateral triangle, not overlapping one another but close enough to make a neat arrangement. Ideally, all should be identical in size, shape and colour distribution. As such perfect matches are rarely found, the choice of bloom for each point of the triangle is important as it may give an impression of greater similarity. A small pillow of moss needs placing at the rear of the vase and the bloom selected as the top point of the triangle should be held against it with its leaves neatly arranged behind the stem. Some moss should be added to hold the stem and leaves in position and then the remaining blooms and associated leaves should be slotted into the front of the vase. More moss should be packed carefully around and between all stems to hold the blooms in the desired position. Again, the packing needs to be firm enough to hold the stems while allowing them to be moved up and down to get each located at the correct height. Three blooms of distinct cultivars in one vase need the same precise arrangement so that size and colour variations look attractive as a whole.

There should be no need to use artificial aids to support stems or hold them in their desired positions. Indeed, many show schedules specifically preclude the use of such aids as wires and sharpened canes. Good cultivation should have produced straight stems of sufficient length and strength. If a stem is weak or lacking in straightness, strong leaves placed down the side will give some support which should be sufficient to give good presentation of the bloom.

It is essential to develop a logical sequence of working when getting the blooms into the vases. Most exhibitors will commence with the blooms that

UNIQUE (4W-Y) is a superb cultivar which has long lasting blooms in the border and a high proportion are of exhibition quality

are to be included in collection classes because once they are staged they are less likely to be knocked or damaged as other blooms are removed from the storage container. Also an initial assessment of heights and arrangement can be made, and reserve blooms can be presented in a consistent arrangement of vase, leaves and styling. Surplus blooms from collection classes will readily slot into single-bloom classes, whereas a bloom staged initially for a single-bloom class may need some restaging if it has to be brought into a collection as a last-minute replacement.

It is surprising the amount of staging space which will be utilised in this way as the exhibit is slowly assembled. Once all this initial staging has been done each vase can be tidied and finally aligned and the debris cleared away. With clean dry hands one can then start to dress each bloom to display it to maximum potential.

MAKING THE MOST OF COLLECTIONS

Any collection of daffodils must be well presented not only to maximise the potential of each bloom but to ensure that the total effect is pleasing enough to attract additional points. There are a number of little devices which taken together will help to make the exhibit look as impressive as possible.

Although it is the blooms which will be subjected to the critical assessment of the judge, the vases in which they are displayed can detract from the impact of the total exhibit. At most shows, the exhibitor will use the range of vases provided and, ideally, all the vases selected for a particular exhibit should be of the same size and colour. Not only does this make it easier to relocate the blooms within the exhibit, it helps to ensure that all blooms are staged in an identical manner. It may take a little extra time at some shows to find a matching set of vases but the effort is well worth while. In staging multi-vase exhibits the blooms must be aligned precisely and whilst this can be achieved with different-sized vases they create an uneven background to the exhibit and an illusion that the presentation is at fault.

The type of staging available for collections varies considerably from show to show. The facility needs to be assessed before any blooms are put into vases so that they can be arranged at a height compatible with the staging. In general terms, the longer the length of stem which can be utilised the better, and this is a generally favoured approach. However, in a collection it may be advantageous to adjust stem lengths so that the overall effect is in keeping

PART OF THE WONDERFUL LEGACY OF DAFFODILS introduced by John Lea. *Top centre* Rubh Mor (2W-OOR) (1971); *top left* Loch Assynt (3W-GWO) (1963); *top right* Loch Rimsdale (2Y-R) (1985); *centre* Ben Hee (2W-W) (1964); *bottom left* Gold Convention (1Y-Y) (1978); *bottom right* Dailmanach (2W-P) (1972)

with the type of staging. If the staging has a backing cloth, the top row of blooms should have the stem length adjusted so that each bloom is seen against the backing material. Blooms which are too tall to be viewed against the backing material may not be seen to advantage, say, against the colouring of walls and, considering that these may be the best blooms in the set, visual impact is lost. It is equally distracting to view a top row of blooms half overlapping the edge of the backing material and it certainly is not giving the public a chance to see the true beauty of the flowers.

Setting the appropriate height for the top row of blooms does not automatically establish the height for the remaining blooms in the set. Very often the drop of the different levels of the staging is uneven and this means that arranging all blooms to a common height creates different gaps between the rows, giving the impression that the exhibit is either top heavy or bottom heavy. The lengths of the stems on each level of the staging need to be adjusted so that when the exhibit is assessed from the front there is an equal gap between each row of blooms and the blooms are set at a height where they can be seen without interruption. A set of twelve blooms is traditionally staged as three rows of four blooms and this necessitates careful alignment so that each vertical row is in a straight line and parallel to its neighbour, with equal distance between each. Other arrangements are possible but tend to use a greater amount of space, for example:

In both these arrangements there is less risk of blooms masking those in the next row back but even greater attention to sizes and colours is needed to present a pleasing effect. Some shows use flat tabling, even for collections; in such cases the lengths of the stems need to be graded from back to front of the exhibit to give the judge a better chance of appreciating each bloom — the tallest stems at the back, slightly shorter in the middle row and a similar further reduction for the front row. There is a limit to the degree of graduation that can be effected sensibly but the effort does enhance the appearance.

When looking at a collection the eye tends to be drawn to the top row of blooms and to the top right-hand corner. The top row is also a greater distance from the viewer and this can make the blooms appear slightly smaller. Thus, in trying to give the impression of balance, the larger blooms should be on the top row; the smaller blooms would normally be on the lowest level of the staging. In assessing the exhibit most judges will start in the top left-hand corner, and location of the best bloom at this point will maximise the initial impact. On the other hand, if the best bloom is at the top right-hand corner, as the last bloom to be examined it will enhance the initial perception of the total row even though the first impact may not be so great. Each bloom will be taken down during judging for assessment but the arrangement of the collection may enhance the effect and command additional points. An absolutely immaculate large-size bloom may have to be left out of the final exhibit if it is too imposing and detracts from the remainder. A balance of size and quality has much to commend it.

Unless the schedule calls for blooms of a particular colour combination a collection should be truly representative of the designated sub-divisions. Twelve blooms from not less than three Divisions, in theory, can be made up in many different ways; however, four blooms from each of Divisions 1, 2 and 3 are more meritorious than ten from Division 1 and one each from Divisions 2 and 3. Equally, twelve blooms with yellow perianths are less meritorious than an equal split between yellow and white perianths. The unwritten convention places more merit upon alternating perianth colour across the rows eg:

y	w	y	w
w	y	w	y
y	w	y	w

For less than twelve blooms the appropriate number of vertical rows should be selected but must retain the alternation of perianth colour. The number of possible permutations is significantly increased when the question of corona colour is introduced. Highly-coloured coronas should be included but too many can give an illusion of imbalance in the total exhibit — an ideal is one red corona per horizontal row. It is not appropriate to talk of colours clashing with one another but some care must be taken to ensure that, for example, a delicate pink is not swamped by being surrounded by intense red cups. This can be effectively done only at the time of setting up the exhibit and may necessitate rearrangements to give the desired balance.

A final appraisal of the exhibit is vital. Check that you have the right number of blooms and the defined coverage of Divisions (especially important if there have been rearrangements and substitutions). Alignment of blooms in rows and lines should be adjusted as appropriate and name-of-bloom labels should be straightened so that they merge into the background. Staging debris often gets dragged onto the benching in the juggling of the arrangement and this makes the exhibit look untidy — so a final cleaning of the bench and the vases may be necessary. If there is a significant time lapse between staging and judging, each vase should be carefully topped up with water and it can be beneficial to give the total exhibit a light spray with clean water. Spraying needs great care and if there is a risk of very low temperatures it may be better omitted.

None of these points will compensate for poor blooms but the creation of a pleasing overall impression is absolutely essential if the thrill of staging a top-notch exhibit is to be attained. Remember that exhibiting can be fun and it is far better to put up a well-presented but unplaced collection than to leave your blooms at home.

SHOWING POTS OF BLOOMS

Many shows include classes for pots, of defined dimensions, containing bulbs in growth. These pots can look very attractive if well grown and with a little care being taken to present them in tasteful style.

Choice of cultivars is important if the blooms are to be well held above the foliage. Cool growing will ensure that the stems do not become too elongated and too weak to support the blooms. A faded or fading bloom will detract from the impression of the total exhibit — better to remove it carefully by cutting just below the spathe so that the stem looks like just another leaf.

Signs of disease or bulb disorders will also lose points. Brown tips to the leaves should be cut off neatly and distorted or discoloured leaves should be cut out at soil level just before staging. If a bulb has failed it is better to remove all traces of it as soon as possible to give time for the remaining growth to occupy the space at bloom level. Occasionally some bulbs will produce a number of secondary small leaves which are difficult to restrain neatly and without risking damage to the other leaves or blooms. Such small growths are better cut off, with a sharp knife, level with the compost so that their removal cannot be detected.

If there is any suspicion of weakness in the stems it is appropriate to tie the growth to keep it upright. Dyed split canes are ideal and the minimum possible number should be used consistent with good support. Surplus length can be cut off so that the canes are concealed within the foliage and not obtrusive. Any material used for tying the growth to the canes again should be unobtrusive, though this might mean retying the plant once it has arrived at the show hall if extra raffia or string put on for transport has to be cut out at the last minute.

It is helpful to identify the particular cultivar being shown. A label that has been in the pot throughout the growing season may be dirty or faded and should be replaced. A new, clean label with neatly-written, legible name will enhance the presentation. Finally, the pot should be clean and here plastic has the advantage over clay. The surface of the compost should be cleared of any germinating weeds and it may be beneficial in close competition to add a top layer of 1/8in (3mm) washed gravel. On the staging the pot should be placed in a suitably-sized plastic saucer so that there are no signs of moisture staining the covering around its base and giving the impression of untidiness.

•7•
Pests and Diseases

Daffodils are, in general terms, healthy plants not prone to too many troubles. Indeed, their ability to come up year after year has given most people the impression that they are not affected by the same range of pests and diseases as other popular garden subjects. However, most judgements on the lack of troubles are made by year upon year comparisons of mass plantings — these are not really valid as odd gaps cannot be seen and last year's crop of blooms cannot be remembered in detail.

Without wishing in any way to discourage the growing of daffodils or to focus too much attention on pests and diseases, it is essential to give some insight into the troubles which can affect the genus. It must be remembered that where daffodils are grown in containers or special beds the regular close inspection of growth is more likely to highlight gaps or distortions which may be the indications of some previously unsuspected problem. Pests can be brought in from many sources and indeed they can jump the fence between neighbouring gardens — they do not differentiate between cultivars but often seem to favour the more expensive novelties in their search for food. Diseases, too, do not really differentiate between cultivars and because they are largely unseen, except for the distortions to growth, they may lurk in peculiar ways until a suitable host plant is available.

Over the years various pests and diseases have come close to eliminating commercial crops of daffodils. Research workers have usually been on hand to identify suitable control techniques though it is somewhat unfortunate that many of them are beyond the scope of the amateur grower, either through cost of equipment or the toxicity of the treatments. Research is continuing and, although it is too early to claim any major breakthrough, some avenues are being identified which may result in the breeding of cultivars with a genetic resistance to some of the more prevalent diseases and this would make them more attractive to commercial growers and for garden display. Tissue culture techniques are also being adopted to clean up stocks of cultivars which have an important bearing on the economy of some areas. Perhaps the most significant example is the development of a virus-free stock of Grand Soleil d'Or, which is a most popular early-flowering cultivar and the backbone of the flower trade of the Isles of Scilly — each stem of the cleansed stock may bear up to twenty florets as compared to the unclean stock which has degenerated to about eight florets. Other cultivars have been cleaned of virus, for example Sealing Wax, and as they become more readily available the true potential of these cultivars will once again be evident. On an amateur scale, tissue culture can be practised but the success rate is discouraging except to those who are proving a technique.

The following summary is limited to the relatively major problems that can and do occasionally arise wherever daffodils are grown.

PESTS

A number of insects have been identified as major pests of daffodils. Whilst they may do fatal damage to the bulb which they have entered or attacked they can also survive from one year to the next and perpetuate the problems.

Large narcissus 'fly'

This particular pest can cause serious problems to a variety of bulbous subjects though it appears to have a marked preference for daffodils: hence it is usually referred to as the large narcissus fly but more correctly it is *Merodon equestris*. The large narcissus fly occurs in most areas where daffodils are grown, though in the UK it appears to be a much more serious problem in the warmer areas such as Cornwall. The adult fly does very little damage to either flowers or bulbs, or foliage; the real harm is done by the maggot (larva) as it scavenges for food in the period up to pupating.

The large narcissus fly resembles a bumble bee in size — up to ¾in (2cm) long — and colour but it has only one pair of wings, characteristic of a fly. Colouring of the adult fly varies but the hairy thorax has defined banding of blackish brown and a lighter colouring which can be yellowish or orange brown. The fly emerges from the pupal state towards the end of the daffodil flowering season, the exact timing being dependent upon the ambient temperatures, and is usually seen just before the blooms fade. Occasionally the fly can be seen earlier in the season where it has come from bulbs that have been forced or grown in a protected environment.

Following mating, each female fly is capable of laying up to 40 eggs though each is deposited singly on the lower parts of daffodil foliage and often in the gaps created between the foliage and compacted soils. The eggs usually hatch after ten days of incubation and the tiny transparent maggot then migrates down the foliage and the outside of the bulb until it can attach itself to the base-plate. It proceeds to tunnel its way through the base-plate and into the fleshy scales of the bulb where it makes itself comfortable and then munches its way through the heart of the bulb, refilling the hollowed-out cavity as it progresses with spongy black body wastes. Usually there is only one maggot in each bulb but if the food supply is inadequate the maggot will move to another host. As the soil, and bulb, temperature drops in autumn so does the activity of the maggot and with the onset of winter most of the damage has been done. At this stage the maggot will usually leave the bulb by the remnants of its neck and once in the soil it will pupate. The pupal stage usually lasts a minimum of sixty days and when the temperature has risen sufficiently the adult fly emerges and hunts for a mate to restart the cycle.

It is perhaps fortunate that only one generation of the large narcissus fly is produced each year, as each maggot will completely destroy one average-sized bulb. In some areas as many as 60 per cent of untreated bulbs can be affected by the fly whereas in cooler areas the proportion may be only 5 per cent.

The damage to the bulbs is really only evident when they have been lifted from the ground and at that time may not be readily identifiable. There may be a suspicion of softness near the neck of the bulb and it may also be possible to identify the telltale hole through the base-plate if the bulbs can be cleaned sufficiently to permit examination. It is much more likely that the damage will be identifiable as the time approaches for replanting — the maggot will have devoured a greater volume of the bulb scales so that the softness of the bulb can be detected by pressure between fingers and thumb.

Once a bulb has been attacked by the large narcissus fly it is virtually impossible to save it. Occasionally, with a very large bulb, some growing points are initiated from the base-plate between undamaged bulb scales and in such cases the bulb will produce a ring of grass-like foliage the following season. Such foliage will feed the tiny bulbs and four years of growth in ideal conditions should get them back to flowering size. If it has been possible to identify the problem early on it may be possible to kill the maggot with a needle inserted through the hole in the base-plate, though it can be a risky business and is only worth attempting where an expensive cultivar is involved. The best course of action with an affected bulb is to destroy it by burning or cut it open so that the maggot can be found and killed before the bulb is disposed of.

It is difficult to control the large narcissus fly during its active season. Attempts can be made to trap the fly but its peculiar jerking flight patterns make this difficult, though the unique high-pitched sound can galvanise most daffodil growers into spells of frantic activity. Where daffodils are being grown in special beds it may be advantageous to hoe the top 2in (5cm) of soil into a very fine tilth so that it can be worked up close to the foliage to make it more difficult for the eggs to be laid sufficiently low down on the leaves. This is a time-consuming exercise that would not be possible on a commercial scale. Some growers advocate the spraying of the foliage with dimethoate every twenty-one days after flowering, but again this is not entirely effective.

Small narcissus fly
Two very similar species of fly which, although they will also attack other subjects, have a preference for daffodils are known collectively as the small narcissus fly. This fly is only about $\frac{1}{3}$in (8mm) long and is usually very dark coloured, almost black, but with a bloom of yellow/orange overlaying the thorax: it can be confused with a common house fly. It is clearly a pest though not so frequently experienced as the large narcissus fly.

Again it is the maggot (larva) which does the damage to the bulbs. Eggs are laid on the foliage at ground level or just below the surface, usually in clusters, and upon hatching the new-born maggots migrate down to the bulb and eat their way into its flesh, usually through the neck. Often where a damaged bulb has been planted the scar tissue will ease the maggots' passage into the bulb scales which are to be devoured. Each bulb can play host to a large number of maggots. The small narcissus fly is well capable of producing two or three generations of offspring each year if the humidity is low and the temperatures high.

Signs of damage are almost identical

to those described for the large narcissus fly, with the exception of the characteristic entry hole through the base-plate, though bulbs which have been attacked early in the season may be very soft at the time of lifting. The best control is by the use of a persistent insecticide and attempts at catching the fly are only rarely successful.

Eelworms (nematodes)

These pests have the potential to infest the total bulb population in a very short time. In fact, in the early 1900s nematodes had caused so much damage that there was a serious risk of the elimination of commercial stocks. Fortunately, research work, led by J. K. Ramsbottom, developed the system of hot water treatment (HWT) of dormant bulbs which is now regarded as the standard preventive and control technique (see pages 33–4).

Nematodes are very tiny organisms not normally visible with the naked eye, so detection of their presence is very difficult in existing stocks or those brought in from other sources. Adult nematodes are only about 1/25in (1 to 2mm) long and resemble thread-like transparent worms, hence the common reference to eelworms. They are parasites living within the host bulb in very large quantities. Tiny eggs are laid and after hatching go through a number of moults as they develop. Breeding can be continuous and rapid where temperatures are in the range 50° to 60°F (10° to 15°C) and the host plant's tissue is alive. This means that nematodes can and do continue to breed even after bulbs have been lifted and are being kept in store. However, if the nematodes cannot migrate from one bulb to another they may kill the bulb because of the high level of infestation and hence die themselves. Nematodes can migrate through soils from a heavily-infested bulb to another which is free of attack and although only a small proportion will

survive the journey they are capable of rapid multiplication once in the new host. Pre-adult nematodes can desiccate or dry out to become a wool-like fibre which is really a dormant stage and which can, if kept free of moisture, exist for many years. In the soil, nematodes cannot survive for more than about twelve months without taking food from a host plant and there are strong indications that several other genera may be able to act as temporary hosts.

Evidence of nematode attack can be seen both during growth and by examination of dry bulbs. Distorted, dwarfed yellow foliage and stems clearly indicate a severe attack. Early signs of infestation are small yellowish swellings on the leaves and stem, perhaps a speckled patch that can best be detected when there is no bright sunlight creating false shadows. Bulbs which are soft when lifted may have been badly affected by nematodes and will deteriorate further during storage, and until fully dry may permit migration from bulb to bulb. An attack can be confirmed if a soft bulb is cut in half transversely, parallel to the base-plate, and it shows dark, almost black, rings between the scales. In an almost fatal attack of nematodes not only will the bulb be very soft to the touch but there will be signs of the base-plate being forced out of the bulb and the whitish nematode wool forming along the fissure — nematodes travel through the spaces between the bulb scales and from one layer to another through the base-plate, thus gentle pressure may have the effect of popping out the base-plate like the cork from a bottle.

Chemical control of nematodes cannot be generally recommended. Some extremely toxic chemicals have been evaluated but their residual effects make them so risky to humans and wildlife that their availability is rigorously controlled. However, there are several chemicals able to control nematodes that have migrated into the soil and which can therefore prevent reinfestation of clean stocks. Such treatments, for example dazomet (sold as 'Basamid'), are not economic for large commercial plantings, though where small stocks of valuable cultivars are being grown the expense may be justified. Soil sterilisers should only be used in the way recommended by the manufacturers. Large quantities of infested bulbs on a commercial scale would justify control of the nematodes by hot water treatment (HWT).

Cultural control is perhaps the only option open to most amateur growers. This depends upon the identification of the presence of nematodes on stems and foliage, through regular inspections from the time the shoots emerge through the soil, and then having the courage and strength of will to rogue out all plants showing signs of attack. Infested plants should be committed to the bonfire immediately. Unless the soil can be sterilised effectively a system of rotation should be adopted to ensure that daffodils are not replanted in the same ground for at least five years and daffodils must be kept away from ground which has been used for other host plants such as onions, beans, peas and strawberries.

Slugs

Although not specifically pests of daffodils, slugs can do a lot of damage that may dishearten the amateur grower. These creatures have some inbuilt instinct which enables them to identify the most expensive cultivar or the rarest species as their preferred source of food. Damage can be to the bulbs, particularly in a damp area or the plunge bed which is being kept damp and cool in the autumn, or to the emerging shoots in the spring, or indeed to the blooms, especially on warm humid evenings.

When lifting pots and containers from their winter quarters make sure that slugs are not attached to the bases and carried into the protected environment where the conditions could encourage them to become active and commence their search for food. Slug pellets, applied to the surface of the soil, can help to control these pests and prevent damage to foliage and blooms. Other, recently developed, soluble chemical treatments which can be watered onto the soil and penetrate to a depth of about 5in (12cm) can give good control and virtually eliminate damage to the bulbs; a good example is 'Noble' which is now available to the amateur.

Aphids

Aphids, commonly referred to as greenfly, only very rarely colonise on daffodil foliage and hence it is not generally recognised that the various species can be classed as a minor pest of the genus. Climatic conditions will generally limit the period of aphid activity to the six to eight weeks immediately preceding foliage die-back. However, in this relatively short time aphids may settle upon the foliage and attempt to feed, which may cause the transmission of virus disease between plants.

Experimental work is still progressing to establish controls over aphid transmission of virus diseases and at the moment the only safe recommendation is to kill any aphids seen on the foliage, probably using a systemic insecticide.

Other pests

There are several other pests which can attack daffodils. However, these are not often found and should not be of too much concern to the ordinary grower. Bulb scale mites, bulb mites, leaf nematodes etc, can cause damage well out of proportion to their size but by adopting good standards of hygiene at all periods, especially during storage, and the roguing out of suspect plants, serious problems should be avoided.

DISEASES

Although the health of the daffodil can be affected by diseases which result from non-infectious sources such as nutrient deficiencies, frost, wind etc, these problems can readily be corrected by cultural techniques. Infectious diseases caused by microbes, such as bacteria, fungi or viruses, are serious problems which can cause major losses of bulbs through total destruction or progressive degeneration. The disease-causing microbes, pathogens, can exist in almost passive states, perhaps in the same way as nematodes, and only become active when they find a susceptible plant and a favourable environment which is usually temperature dependent.

A whole catalogue of diseases has been identified, though of these only three or four have commercial significance or need to be of concern to the amateur grower.

Basal rot

This is a fungus disease, identified as *Fusarium oxysporum F narcissi*, which takes its common name from its ability to cause the base-plate of the bulb to rot away. It is generally assumed that the fungus is specific to narcissi, though there are suggestions that it can be carried by other subjects or even survive in soil for a number of years until it finds a host plant. Not all narcissus cultivars are equally susceptible to basal rot: the commercial cultivar Golden Harvest (1Y-Y) appears highly susceptible, as do those white cultivars with Madame de Graff (1W-W) in their pedigrees, whereas Saint Keverne (2Y-Y) is almost resistant and appears to pass this attribute to its offspring.

Basal rot develops very rapidly during the period following harvesting and whilst the bulbs are in store. It usually becomes apparent about three weeks after lifting as a softening of the bulb accompanied by a reddish-brown discoloration in the region of the ring of old root scars. The rot gradually spreads through the base-plate and into the fleshy part of the bulb. The symptoms are similar to those of an eelworm (nematode) attack but instead of displaying concentric rings the rot will more or less affect all of the bulb tissue which becomes brown/greyish brown and amorphous. The rot gradually spreads upwards until all that is remaining is a desiccated shell filled with rotted material, though occasionally there are signs of a pinkish-white fungus between the desiccated scales.

It is very likely that the fungus enters the bulb through wounds in the base-plate, caused by emerging roots or by damage during cleaning. Temperatures above 54°F (12°C) cause development of the fungus though it would appear to be most rapid at about 77°F (25°C). It is known that the fungus can survive below 54°F (12°C) but its rate of spread is reduced as the temperatures fall. Good, cool storage conditions are therefore important.

Suspect bulbs should be destroyed by burning. However, some bulbs harbouring the fungus may not show the symptoms and may be replanted to produce in the following year a weakly growth with dwarfed yellowish leaves. Such weakly developing plants should be rogued out as they will never recover their health and can infect the soil.

Various researchers and enthusiastic amateurs have arrived at the conclusion that basal rot can be best controlled by

Basal rot has attacked the right-hand off-set and is progressing through the remaining parts, resulting in weak, distorted growth

use of fungicides. A benomyl dip, eg 'Benlate', is effective, but best results would be achieved by the following programme:

1 Lift bulbs, carefully avoiding damage to base-plate or scales, before the roots have faded.
2 Within twelve hours of lifting, dip bulbs for fifteen minutes in a 0.5 per cent formalin solution (4 teaspoons eg 40 per cent formaldehyde per gallon of water, 1 to 200 dilution).
3 Dry the bulbs very quickly and thoroughly, especially ensuring the gaps/spaces in double- and triple-nosed bulbs are not retaining water. Drying in sunlight may cause temperatures to rise and give the fungus time to establish itself; a forced draught in a cool place is safer.
4 Store the bulbs in a cool, well-ventilated area.
5 Check the bulbs regularly and discard those showing symptoms of disease.
6 Immediately prior to planting dip the bulbs in a benomyl solution, eg 'Ben-

late' at 5 per cent dilution, and replant whilst still wet.

Some concern is rightly being voiced that the fusarium fungus may develop a resistance to systemic fungicides, such as benomyl, if they are used too frequently. The programme outlined above should not lead to this problem if bulbs are left down for two years; however, if annual lifting is practised the preplanting dip should be omitted every third year or formalin used as a substitute. Recent research is showing that thiobenzol has a good effect for controlling basal rot and could be a valuable alternative to benomyl as a preplanting dip.

Cultural techniques can also have beneficial effects and help to control the spread of basal rot. Where possible, practise crop rotation so that daffodils are not replanted in the same ground for at least five years. Plant in raised beds to ensure good drainage which will make conditions less favourable for the fungus to exist in the soil. To keep bulbs cool at planting time, thereby restricting development of the fungus, they should be planted with at least 6in (15cm) of soil over them. The use of low-nitrogen fertilisers produces harder growth in the bulbs which appears to make it more difficult for the fungus to establish itself and spread. Soil fumigation may curtail the spread of basal rot, but the technique is usually beyond the resources of the amateur grower.

By the combination of chemical control and cultural techniques it should be possible to reduce losses from basal rot to some 1 per cent, and at this level bulb increase should ensure a steady build-up of stocks.

Leaf scorch

This is a serious disease which affects the leaves of the plant and limits their ability to produce food so that there is progressive degeneration of the bulb. It is another fungus, *Stagonospora curtisii*, which appears to be specific to daffodils and which needs a host bulb to survive the winter.

The fungus is usually on the neck area of the bulb and as the growing tips of the leaves emerge they become infected. The infection develops very rapidly and is seen as a reddish-brown scorch, similar to that caused by frost, which gradually spreads down the leaves. There can be secondary infection caused by splashing with rain when the fungus is carried onto other leaves, showing as oval reddish-brown stains, each with a dark rim. Infected leaves, as they die back, allow the fungus to travel, or be carried, down to the neck of the bulb where it again survives the winter.

Fungicide treatment, by dipping the bulbs as recommended for basal rot, will control the spread of disease. However, additional control can be effected by spraying the foliage with benomyl, eg 'Benlate', when the shoots are some 3in (7cm) tall, just before bud-break and about one week after flowering. If there are signs of leaf scorch the laborious process of removing the infected tips, which should be burned, will stop secondary infections and limit the damage to the rest of the leaves, and will make the spraying programme more effective.

Yellow stripe

More correctly this disease is called narcissus yellow stripe virus (NYSV) and is the most commonly encountered virus disease. It is specific to daffodils and causes rapid degeneration of the bulbs because it drastically impairs the ability of the leaves to photosynthesise.

NYSV is clearly evident as the leaves begin to emerge and shows as a bright yellow vertical striping. It can be detected when the leaves are quite tiny but is more readily seen when the leaves are about 6in (15cm) tall and especially when they are studied in dull lighting.

It is unfortunate that there is no known remedy for NYSV. The only

thing that can be done, once the disease has been identified, is to dig out the affected bulb and destroy it by burning. This roguing should be done irrespective of the original cost of the bulb to ensure that the virus is not carried by vectors — nematodes or aphids — to other foliage.

Very often newly-acquired bulbs in their first year of growth show signs that may be reminiscent of NYSV. This may be a similar virus that is carried within the bulb and which has become evident only because of the change in the soil, in particular its pH and fertility, or the change in flowering season. Isolation of these bulbs, say, in pots, for at least one season, may mean that healthy normal growth again masks the symptomatic expression of a less critical virus infection.

Other diseases

Less widely-encountered diseases include:

White streak (syn Silver Stripe): another specific virus that can be identified by whitish vertical striping on the leaves and which becomes evident following flowering. There is no known treatment and affected bulbs should be rogued out and burnt.

Smoulder (Botryotinia narcissicola): a fungus disease that affects both leaves and bulbs. The leaf symptoms are crisp black tips or complete rotting and wilting of the plant at ground level following a peculiar curling degeneration. On the bulb there are flat, round to oval, black plates, about 1/8in (1 to 2mm) in diameter. The spread of this disease is not clearly understood and may be dependent upon nematodes. Fungicide dipping, as for basal rot, appears to be effective.

Constant vigilance is necessary to watch for signs of disease. In general terms those showing leaf symptoms require urgent action once seen; those of virus origin must be rogued out and others should trigger a programme of spraying.

118

•8•
Breeding and Breeders

When left to natural agencies daffodils only rarely set seed. However, it is through seeds that new cultivars are created and, in the case of species, that a quicker reproduction of stocks is obtained.

Seed produced on recognised cultivars will not create plants which are identical to the seed parent but each seed will be a unique hybrid. The seed will inherit characteristics from both the seed parent and the pollen parent and the majority of these hybrids will not have characteristics which are an improvement on existing registered cultivars. In general terms, the pollen parent will have the greatest influence upon the colours transmitted into the seed, whereas the seed parent will have the greatest influence on the form and classification of the offspring.

In the catalogues of the specialist suppliers, each cultivar will have its known parentage recorded as: White Star bred from Rashee cross Empress of Ireland; or as White Star (Rashee×Empress of Ireland). In this case the pollen parent of White Star was Empress of Ireland and the seed parent was Rashee. Thus, in keeping records of any breeding work undertaken this approach should be adopted for consistency and ready understanding.

PRODUCING SEEDS

The mechanics of producing seed are fairly simple. An open flower which is identified as a suitable seed parent should be selected and the stigma of this flower should then have pollen from the chosen pollen parent applied to it. The transfer of pollen is best done by removing a complete anther from the pollen parent, using a pair of tweezers, and then gently rubbing the anther across the selected stigma. Pollen can also be transferred with a small, soft-haired brush but this must be cleaned in methylated spirits between each cross if one is to be absolutely certain about the parentage of any seeds. The transfer is best done about mid-day and when it is bright and sunny, though it can be done with some success at other times. Some people advocate applying sugar solution or saliva to the stigma to assist with adhesion of pollen but if the flower is sufficiently mature such assistance is not necessary. The selected anther should be well developed so that there is enough pollen avail-

able for transfer to three or four stigmas. As soon as a stigma has been polli-
nated the flower stem should be tied loosely to a cane and labelled to record
the cross which was made.

Where the pollination has been successful the seedpod will gradually
resume an upright position as the flower fades, and get larger as the seeds
develop. (Sometimes a seedpod will appear to be viable but then fade because
there has been a false pregnancy.) The pod will continue to develop through
until midsummer (about nine or ten weeks) and then the seeds will ripen. It
is important to check the seedpods at regular intervals for signs that they are
almost ripe, usually detected as a change from green to yellow and then
brown, or by the fact that the seeds can be heard to rattle when the pod is
gently shaken. Alternatively, the withered remnant of the flower should be
gently tweaked — it will pull away if the pod is ripe and preparing to burst
open. Where the seeds are from a planned cross it is advisable to remove the

POLLINATION requires a little patience. An anther from another cultivar is being held in
tweezers and dabbed onto the stigma of the chosen seed parent. It is rarely necessary to remove
the anthers from the potential seed parent, due to the low incidence of natural pollination.
After pollination, the stem of the flower should be fastened to a split cane and have a label
attached to record the source of the pollen and the date it was crossed

pod from the stem before it bursts and to allow it to dry and burst in an envelope so that seeds will not be lost or scattered by the vibration of the stem. A ripened seedpod may contain one seed or a hundred, the number being influenced by the characteristics of the seed parent, the conditions in which fertilisation took place or by the state of cultivation of the bulb.

When planting daffodil seed one will not get the same instant response as with the planting of annuals. From seed production to flowering can take four or more years, as the ability to produce a first flower depends upon the grower's skills at producing a bulb large enough to initiate and develop the stem and bloom. So in sowing seed there is going to be a long wait until the first flowers are seen and even then a lot of ugly ducklings may create disappointment. However, if a few seeds are collected and planted each year there will be something new to appreciate every year following the initial waiting period.

Some crosses are more likely to produce acceptable flowers than others but it is largely a case of trial and error. Kilworth (2W-GRR) × Arbar (2W-O) and Chinese White (3W-GWW) × Green Island (2W-GWY) have produced a number of good flowers but, even so, the percentage returns are very low; perhaps some of the success of these crosses has been due to the very large numbers of seed sown over a period of years. Only a very small percentage of the seeds will produce flowers that are worth growing on into usable stocks but the whole exercise creates an additional interest for most growers who like to experiment. A careful study of the specialist catalogues will help to identify the cultivars which have been useful as pollen or seed parents and this should help the beginner to plan experimental crosses. It is essential to have a method when dabbing pollen about as a casual approach is less likely to be successful. Ideally, the best of the seedlings should be selected for particular characteristics and then used for future breeding so that a new line may be available as an alternative to repeating what has been done before.

At all times the objective should be to use the best available cultivars, even if it means begging a bloom or a stamen of a cultivar which you cannot afford to grow. Most exhibitors will be prepared at the end of a show to donate a bloom to help. Pollen has a fairly long viability provided it is stored in cool, dry conditions and a small airtight container with a segregated supply of silica gel, which is a useful aid and allows pollen from an early-flowering cultivar to be kept viable whilst you wait for a later cultivar to become ready to accept it. Such supplies of pollen, in their special containers, should be stored in a corner of a domestic refrigerator.

BULB DEVELOPMENT

Once seed has been obtained it should be sown as early as possible in a container which has enough depth to allow a good root run: 7 or 8in (17 or 20cm) pots are ideal and they should be filled to within 1in (2.5cm) of the top with a John Innes type of compost equivalent to No 2 or No 3. Wooden boxes can also be used provided that adequate drainage holes are created. The compost must be firmed to produce a level surface onto which the seeds should be carefully placed so that they are 1in (2.5cm) apart in each direction. A covering of not more than ½in (1cm) of compost should then be placed over the seeds, firmed down and watered to check that the completed container is free draining. The container should then be stood, after having a suitable label inserted and a top dressing of fine gravel, to deter slugs, in a sheltered spot so that it gets a minimum of sun and is protected from the extremes of the weather. Regular checks should be made to ensure that the container does not dry out and also to watch against waterlogging. A cover of wire netting is a useful precaution against birds or animals disturbing the seeds or subsequent growth. Initial growth may be expected after some three to four months ie by about the shortest day, but the rate of germination will depend upon the freshness of the seed at planting time and will be at best not more than 95 per cent. The first growth will be the single round seed leaf which will continue to grow and be viable through to the following summer when it will die back into the bulbil. The contractile root action will have taken the bulbil down into the compost to a more appropriate depth.

Once the first season's growth has died back it is advisable to remove the top ½in (1cm) of compost from the container and replace it with a fresh supply equivalent to John Innes No 3. If this is done carefully there should be no risk of damage to the small bulbils but any weed or weed seed from the surface will be removed so that there is less competition for the available food. Some ungerminated seeds may be lost but it is better to take proper care of those that have grown and to replenish some fertiliser in the container. The surface covering of sharp gravel should be replaced to deter slugs from venturing across the container and devouring new growth.

Growth may again be expected to be visible during winter, dependent to some extent upon the prevailing weather conditions. Two typical, but small-scale, daffodil leaves can be expected in this second season. The container should again be checked regularly to ensure that the compost does not dry out and the application of weak solutions of liquid fertilisers should be made about one month apart during the spring. The leaves will fade, at about the same time as the leaves from mature bulbs die back, as the bulbils prepare for

---

MERLIN (3W-GYR) is a remarkably consistent cultivar introduced by J. Lionel Richardson in 1956. It has received many awards from the Royal Horticultural Society (including an FCC as a cultivar for garden display) and wins many prizes at local and national daffodil shows

their dormant period. Once the leaves have begun to fade, but whilst they are still recognisable, the container should be carefully emptied. The bulbils must be gathered together ready for cleaning and storage, with those from each cross being kept separated from others. During storage the bulbils should be treated exactly as their full-scale equivalents but perhaps greater care should be exercised in removal of roots as their tiny base-plates are quite delicate. It is sensible to dip the bulbils for fungal disease and against the narcissus fly but the hot water treatment is too severe (see Chapter 2). The bulbils from each cross should be counted for comparison with the number of seeds originally planted.

After storage, and preferably by late summer, the bulbils should be planted in well-prepared open ground. They will remain in these conditions for at least three years and so they should be planted about 5 to 6in (12 to 15cm) apart in each direction. The more space that can be allowed the better, as this will assist when a particularly promising cultivar needs to be lifted for growing on without disturbing those that are being given more time to prove their potential or to reach flowering size. The beds of seedlings need perhaps more attention than those of standard cultivars to keep them free of competing weeds and to ensure that a good supply of water and liquid fertiliser is provided to give the best possible chance of reaching a flowering-size bulb. There are no short cuts, as nature requires a minimum period of time to develop a flowering-size bulb, and therefore the best of attention will result in the flower being attained that much earlier, hopefully in the fourth year of growth.

The first flowers from the new bulbs will not be a true indication of the full potential of the unique new cultivar. However, there should be a sufficient indication to permit selections to be made. Few are likely to be improvements on existing cultivars or to be potential breeding stock and unless there is unlimited space available it really does pay to be ruthlessly selective, retaining only the ones that are exceptional. From this point on the bulbs will multiply by natural division and any which have been selected can then be built up into useful stocks. Where there is a cultivar that shows real promise it may be advisable, as soon as a viable off-set has been produced, to pass it to someone else so that if a disaster strikes then the total stock is not lost. Also, once a small stock exists, other systems of propagation could be investigated to speed up the process of developing a good supply of bulbs (see pages 35–7).

BREEDERS IN NORTHERN IRELAND have built up an unparalleled reputation for introducing many fine cultivars. *Top left* Newcastle (1W-Y) from W. J. Dunlop (1957); *top right* Silent Valley (1W-W) from T. Bloomer (1964); *centre* Standfast (1Y-Y) from T. Bloomer (1982); *bottom left* Doctor Hugh (3W-GOO) from B. S. Duncan (1975); *bottom right* Silent Cheer (3W-YYR) from T. Bloomer (1964)

Many of the species can also be raised from seed as they will generally come true to type and the sowing of seed permits a more rapid build-up of stocks. The technique is identical to the approach outlined above, except that as the majority of the species have only quite small bulbs they may remain in the same container from the initial sowing of the seed through to the achievement of the first flowers, with sensible application of fertilisers at appropriate times.

BREEDERS

The famous plant collectors of the Victorian age became infatuated with the daffodil. Their zeal led to the development of the genus and the styles of flowers which are familiar to us today. A special Daffodil Conference, sponsored by the Royal Horticultural Society (RHS) in 1884, consolidated the work of the pioneers, such as Dean William Herbert and William Leeds, who had clearly demonstrated that many of the new species were essentially natural hybrids. This gave new opportunities which were seized upon by many people as a rewarding pastime and saw selective hybridisation begin to improve the range and colouring of daffodils.

The early breeders really committed themselves wholeheartedly to their quest for better cultivars. They quickly adopted the idea of working from what was thought to be the best available material and raised quite enormous numbers of seedlings from which only a very small proportion were selected for further breeding. The Reverend George Engleheart was typical of the period and was responsible for introducing many new cultivars in a wide range of styles; his memory is perpetuated through the Challenge Cup awarded annually by the RHS for the best exhibit of twelve cultivars raised by the exhibitor. Peter Barr was another tireless worker towards improvements in daffodils and for collecting the various species; his enthusiasm was infectious. It is fitting that the Peter Barr Memorial Cup is awarded annually at the discretion of the RHS Council to a person who has made a major contribution to the development of the daffodil.

The Midland Daffodil Society (the forerunner of the Daffodil Society) was established in 1898 in Birmingham, to be responsible for an annual exhibition and for developing interest in the genus. Many of the trophies awarded at the Daffodil Society annual competitions bear the names of the pioneers who gave such a wonderful legacy of improvements and laid the foundations for the cultivars we now enjoy each spring. The early competitions of the Daffodil Society clearly reflected the scale of gardens which were then considered fairly normal (one class called for fifty cultivars and not less than three stems of each). At some of the early shows it was not uncommon for individual amateur exhibitors to put over five hundred blooms into competition.

126

Although times have changed, daffodils, in different styles, can be truly accommodated in modern gardens.

Each year the RHS, as the International Registration authority, now adds some two hundred new cultivars to its register. Many of these new cultivars are created by keen amateurs, as well as commercial concerns, from many parts of the world, notably England, Northern Ireland, United States of America, New Zealand, Tasmania and Holland. The total register now embraces about 24,000 names. With such a listing it is perhaps understandable that some cultivars have virtually faded away whilst others are inevitably so similar that even the experts have difficulty in assigning correct names to particular blooms. From the new cultivars named and registered each year only a very small proportion will achieve widespread popularity and recognition because of their precision of colour, form, vigour and resistance to disease or weather, and will become indispensable in gardens or on the show-bench: the majority will only achieve transient popularity.

Over the years there have been very few cultivars that have achieved lasting popularity. Perhaps the classic is King Alfred (1Y-Y), which was registered in 1889 and that year was awarded a First Class Certificate due to its vastly superior standard of perianth and colour. Bulbs of King Alfred were changing hands at £10 each at the turn of the century and it has now become a major commercial cultivar distributed by the hundreds of tons each year. In fact, King Alfred is the only daffodil name that is quoted and recognised by most gardeners and is practically synonymous with a yellow trumpet daffodil. (Some experts maintain that King Alfred was virtually wiped out by disease and that the marketing of other yellow trumpets has perpetuated the name.)

The trumpet, or corona, is a characteristic of most daffodils and as a result of the breeding work initiated in the nineteenth century the range of colours and forms has been transformed. Most of the species daffodils have yellow or whitish coronas but the intense red of the various N poeticus sub-species has been extended into a whole range of highly-coloured cultivars. The first breakthrough of red colouring came in 1898 with the introduction of Will Scarlet, a bloom with narrow twisted petals but a spreading well-coloured corona. A new era in red-coloured cultivars came in 1923 with the registration of Fortune by Walter Ware — an appropriate name for a cultivar which sold at £50 per bulb for many years and received most awards possible in England and Holland for exhibition, garden display and cut flower purposes. It has been surpassed for colouring and form by many of its offspring but remains of tremendous importance for the cut-flower trade and quantity sales of dry bulbs.

A further important colour development was the achievement of a true pink in the corona. Mrs R. O. Backhouse was registered in 1923 and was the first pink of any consequence, and can still cause a sensation when seen in quantity. The cultivar lacks refinement due to a very narrow perianth but has an important place in the history of the modern daffodil. Pink colouring is now extremely popular and the more recently-introduced cultivars, such as Dailmanach registered in 1972, still command relatively high prices but have a constitution and perfection of form that will assure them of a long future on the show-bench and for garden display.

The cultivars which are in existence are living tributes to the skills and dedication of their raisers, and in assessing the contribution of each of the famous names there must be a degree of personal preference showing through. The following comments record some of the notable achievements of a few of the well-respected raisers of the modern daffodils, though the work of many others has been of great value in the quest for perfection.

The Reverend G. H. Engleheart

George Engleheart (1851–1936) was the first of the breeders really to aim towards the perfection of form which we now regard as normal. At the time he was creating his new daffodils, at Andover in Hampshire and later near Salisbury, Wiltshire, the range of cultivars available to him was very limited, but by careful selection from his seedlings he was able to make major advances. Few of his introductions are still available, though many of them appear in the pedigrees of the current favourites. Will Scarlet (2W-O/R) is quite an insignificant flower except for its intensity of colouring but it is the forerunner of the intense reds and oranges which we now expect. Beersheba (1W-W) remains a useful white trumpet and created the basis of the modern giant whites. Sea Green (9W-GGR) is still one of the finest poeticus hybrids and is one of the many of this type that were raised; it is still extremely useful for breeding Division 9 cultivars.

J. L. Richardson

Based in Waterford, Eire, J. Lionel Richardson (1890–1961) started by buying in examples of the best cultivars and proceeded to make major advances across most of the Divisions. He is perhaps best remembered for his brightly-coloured flowers and in particular those which came from the crossing of Kilworth (2W-GRR) with Arbar (2W-O): notably Avenger (2W-R), Hotspur (2W-R) and Orion (2W-O), all of which still appear on the show-bench and which are impressive for garden display. Other colours benefited from his attentions: Kingscourt (1Y-Y) is still a force to be reckoned with and is unbeatable in the garden, whilst other all-yellow flowers include Arctic Gold (1Y-Y), Viking (1Y-Y), the slightly more expensive Golden Aura (2Y-Y), and Great Expectations (2Y-Y). The double daffodils were vastly improved with a whole range named after islands, such as Fiji (4Y-Y), Tahiti (4Y-R) and Hawaii (4Y-R), all marvellous for shows and displays. There are more recent introductions coming forward as serious contenders for attention, such as Unique (4W-Y), Gay Challenger (4W-R) and Gay Kybo (4W-O). Some all-white flowers were bred and, although they were overshadowed by the work of Guy Wilson, such delights as Verona (3W-W) and Snowcrest (3W-GWW) still grace the garden today and occasionally appear on the show-bench. A considerable programme of work was done to develop the 'pinks' and of particular note are Salmon Trout (2W-P), which was the first really refined flower of a true pink colouring, Rainbow (2W-WWP), still a most reliable rimmed cultivar, and the pure-coloured recent introductions such as Fair Prospect (2W-P) and, the jewel in the crown, Gracious Lady (2W-P).

Some of the cultivars were sold as stocks when it was thought that they were not good enough to be named and fortunately they have been rescued; a typical example being Grand Prospect (2Y-W) which is now regarded as the most reliable reversed bicolour generally available. The list could be almost endless as there were literally hundreds of cultivars given names. Following his death in 1961, after fifty years of breeding work, Richardson's stocks were maintained by his charming wife who also produced some wonderful new flowers. It would be very difficult to identify the best cultivar introduced by the Richardsons but if forced to try I would have to choose between Merlin (3W-YYR) (First Class Certificate in 1976 for garden decoration), for its sheer consistency and clarity of colouring, Falstaff (2Y-R) (FCC in 1968), as a wonderful example of the colouring and form that was achieved through dedication to perfection, and Unique (4W-Y) (FCC 1980), as the one that nearly got away.

G. L. Wilson

Guy L. Wilson (1886–1962) is often regarded as the originator of the modern white daffodils and was for many years the serious rival of Lionel Richardson. Being based at Broughshane, Ballymena, Northern Ireland, the breeding work was particularly favoured by a suitable climate. Many crosses were undertaken though the majority of the resultant named cultivars were white trumpets. Such impressive flowers as Vigil (1W-W), Cantatrice (1W-W) and Queenscourt (1W-W) were introduced and such was their quality that they are still used for exhibition and, with their increased availability, for impressive garden displays. Panache (1W-W), though raised by Guy Wilson, was ultimately registered by F. E. Board and although it has had some show successes it has never been really outstanding. Could it be that the original decision not to register was indeed correct? Perhaps the best white trumpet raised by Guy Wilson is Empress of Ireland (1W-W) (Award of Merit, 1956) a cultivar that still produces blooms capable of the Best in Show award and one which has tremendous size and a wonderful refinement even when grown for garden display. Fortunately it has also proved to be a first-class parent giving, amongst others, Burntollet (1W-W), Ladybank (1W-W), Silent Valley (1W-GWW) and White Star (1W-W).

Other colours did receive some attention over the years though the majority of the cultivars never quite managed to compete with those of Lionel Richardson. Passionale (2W-P), however, is one of the finest pinks now readily available and though it has been superseded for top level exhibition work it is a real tribute to Guy Wilson's dedication. Another pink, Drumboe (2W-P), has a remarkable grace of form and, though it is variable in its colouring, still sets a yardstick against which the newer introductions must be judged.

Wilson's successes with white cultivars in other sub-divisions must be mentioned and some daffodil historians rate them amongst his finest introductions. Slemish (2W-GWW but shown as 1W-W) was registered in 1930 and reigned supreme for many years having received an AM for exhibition in 1935, an FCC in 1939 and honours at Haarlem, Holland. The silky smooth Ave (2W-W) and the consistent Easter Moon (2W-GWW) have been wonderful show flowers and parents and are still delightful in the garden. Of the small cupped cultivars Chinese White (3W-GWW) is peerless and achieved an impressive array of awards as a consequence of its dramatic breakthrough in size and texture — attributes which it passed to its progeny.

Guy Wilson built a tremendous reputation for his ability to assess a flower and to pass his love of daffodils to other people. It is therefore most fitting that the Northern Ireland growers established a memorial planting of daffodils, later classified as the national collection, in honour of the lovely flowers which he created. A memorial vase is also now fiercely contested at the RHS Show with a demanding requirement of six vases of three blooms of all-white daffodils.

J. S. B. Lea

The first tentative steps towards breeding were taken by John Lea (1911–84) in the 1940s at his home in Stourport, Worcestershire, and followed the general pattern of working from the best commercially available cultivars. John Lea never planted large quantities of seeds in any year but was extremely selective of both seed and pollen parent and kept impeccable records of all his attempted crosses. The fact that he almost established a monopoly of the Engleheart Cup (ten consecutive wins from 1975, and twelve in total) bears witness to the success of his method and his ability to identify a good cultivar and good parents. He sometimes allowed a cultivar that was later to prove of value to the exhibitor to escape, the notable examples being Canisp (2W-W), Stourbridge (2Y-YYR), more recently Liverpool Festival (2Y-O) and Colleygate (3W-GYR), but none of these really rivalled his first selections. Some of the earlier registrations are now proving to be ideal cultivars for providing intense spots of colour in the garden, typical examples being Loch Owskeich (2Y-O) and Loch Stac (2Y-R).

Most of Lea's cultivars have really good substance and colour and will find niches in the plantings of daffodil growers for many years to come. In selecting specific cultivars it is inevitable that the majority will be those of rich colouring. Loch Hope (2Y-R) (First Class Certificate, 1981) is a splendidly refined cultivar that is a real show-bench flower and potential border belle, though to some people it has a corona of unacceptable or unusual shape. Creagh Dubh (2O-R) is a more recent introduction but it has instant appeal because of the intense orange colouring of the perianth and it appears to have great potential for breeding. Gold Convention (1Y-Y) is an impeccable flower of rich golden shades; though registered as a trumpet it does in some conditions fail to meet the necessary measurements whilst setting a very high standard for others to emulate. Of similar form and substance is Silver Convention (1W-W) which is regarded by some as a near-perfect flower until they see White Convention (1W-W) which is, in all but colour, identical to the more famous gold form. Achduart (3Y-R) is proving to be one of the most consistent cultivars available to the exhibitor (three times best bloom at the RHS show) and has a purity and depth of colour not usually associated with this sub-division.

Perhaps the biggest breakthrough came with the registration of Dailmanach (2W-P), which has a perfection of form and clarity of colour to make it an outstanding flower. Dailmanach is still only available in the quantities to satisfy exhibitors and breeders but it will ultimately be a first-class garden flower as it holds itself so well above the foliage. There have been many well-coloured flowers in other sub-divisions, such as Loch Brora (2W-O), Cairn Toul (3W-ORR) and Loch Coire (3W-R), and each will clearly have an influence upon our future daffodils and be a fitting reminder of the painstaking work which brought the significant advances. On his death in 1984 John Lea left a wonderful legacy of flowers and many seedlings that may yet produce another breakthrough of colour or form.

D. and J. W. Blanchard

Two generations of Blanchards have been involved in a successful romance with daffodils. Both David, between 1925 and his death in 1968, and his son, John who commenced daffodil breeding in 1954, have done much to ensure that even the 'minor' Divisions have benefited from dedicated breeding carried out at Blandford in Dorset. This is in addition to their identification of clones of the species that have particular merit. The miniatures have been enhanced by a carefully developed programme and we now have such delights as Icicle (5W-W) and Pequenita (7Y-Y) which because of their relatively slow rate of multiplication may be restricted to the alpine house for many years before they enhance the rockeries of most gardeners.

Other wonderful flowers from the lower Divisions are Arish Mell (5W-W) and Tuesday's Child (5W-Y), both being graceful in form and yet robust garden flowers. One of the earlier standard cultivars which the Blanchards introduced was Karamudli (1W-Y) and although it cannot compete for colour contrast with some of the more recent novelties it has a perfection of form that should be emulated in many other subdivisions. Some cultivars of note are Purbeck (3W-YYO), Ferndown (3Y-Y), Ashmore (2W-GWW) and Kimmeridge (3W-YYO), the last being perhaps the best example of a glistening perianth yet produced. Latterly, John has been exhibiting some very interesting doubles which promise to give a new dimension to a Division which has been so sadly neglected.

A. Gray

We are fortunate that Alec Gray (1895–1986), based at Camborne, Cornwall, concentrated his love and attentions upon the miniature daffodils. Although many of the cultivars are slow to increase they are becoming more readily available, thanks to twin scaling. Tête-à-Tête (6Y-O) (First Class Certificate, 1962) is a wonderful all-yellow cyclamineus type which usually has two, sometimes three, blooms per stem and its robustness in most situations makes it a very popular choice for the rockery and for decorative pans. A charming triandus hybrid, April Tears (5Y-Y) (FCC Haarlem, 1957), which produces up to five dainty all-yellow heads on each stem, is now becoming very popular and is fortunately available from a number of sources. Of more limited availability, though delightful flowers, are Xit (3W-W), a glistening small cup, Flomay (6W-WWP), a rarity, shy to bloom, with its buff-pink rim to the corona, and Bobbysoxer (7Y-YYO), a delightful jonquil. Segovia (3W-Y) is perhaps my personal favourite with its delicacy and impeccable form which contribute to show-bench success.

C. F. Coleman

Cyril Coleman (1892–1980) is a name synonymous with the development of the cyclamineus hybrids. Some of his early introductions, from his gardens at Cranbrook in Kent, are extremely graceful and prolific plants that fit well into border and rockeries for long-lasting displays of colour. They are also capable of producing the perfection of bloom necessary for the show-bench. Dove Wings (6W-Y), Jenny (6W-W) and Charity May (6Y-Y) are a trio of indispensable cultivars suitable for most purposes from the famous Mitylene (2W-Y) × cyclamineus cross. Many other cultivars were introduced and provided the basis for some of the current developments, such as Andalussia (6Y-O), which are now becoming generally available.

131

Mrs B. Abel Smith

Barbara Abel Smith was initiated into the cultivation of daffodils in 1946 by George H. Johnson, who was himself responsible for many of the cultivars that have not only achieved show-bench success but have been of great commercial importance. Mrs Abel Smith has concentrated her breeding on Divisions 1, 2 and 3 and has introduced many novelties from her lovely plantings at Letty Green, Hertford following her first crossings in 1959. Some interesting early-flowering cultivars have been released, for example Brabazon (1Y-Y) which has the style and growth to be a commercial cut-flower and Willow Green (1W-Y), popular for many uses. Park Springs (3W-WWY) is regarded by many as the best flower introduced and it continues to take Best in Show awards with surprising regularity. More recently, April Love (1W-W) has been recognised as a wonderfully consistent cultivar that does well in pots and the garden; unfortunately it is not universally popular as the perianth appears floppy, but in reality it has great substance. A lot of effort has been directed towards the improvement of pink-cupped cultivars but so far a really pink Division 3 has not emerged, though there have been some near misses. My preferences are for Pink Panther (2W-GPP) and Upper Broughton (2W-GWP) as each represents a positive development of clear pink colourings.

F. E. Board

Also following the established path of commencing with the best of the commercially-available cultivars was Fred Board of Darley Dale, Derbyshire. Board was in his forties when he commenced his hybridising activities in 1948 and was just beginning to see the results of his efforts by his death in 1965. In the twenty years since his death a number of his cultivars have been introduced into commerce and still compete at the highest exhibition standards. A particular favourite is Shining Light (2Y-ORR), which is extremely consistent and ideal for three blooms per vase. Golden Vale (1Y-Y) and Strines (2Y-Y) are two all-yellow cultivars that are always in demand and which can, and do, compete at the highest level.

It is perhaps for the all-white cultivars that Fred Board is most noted and his Broomhill (2W-W) (First Class Certificate, 1974), Dover Cliffs (2W-W) and Misty Glen (2W-GWW) still have an excellence of form that is difficult to surpass. Relatively large numbers of seeds were sown each year as he tried to make up for his late initiation into daffodils and lines were beginning to emerge before fate intervened and dictated that they were not to be developed to their full potential. Altruist (3O-R) is now the most often seen, and readily available, near-red flower that serves as a colourful reminder of one of the characters of the UK daffodil scene.

W. A. Noton

Another English breeder, greatly influenced by Fred Board, is Tony Noton who as a true amateur carries on the quest for something better from his home in Oakham, Leicestershire. Although his principal reputation is as a highly successful exhibitor his breeding, commenced in the early 1960s, has been gifted. As a result of his efforts we have the charming Citronita (3Y-Y), which is one of the most consistent all-yellow small-cupped flowers, well capable of challenging for the highest awards at national shows. A range of all-white cultivars has recently been released to complement Pearly King (1W-W), and Noton's reputation will be carried forward with such fine blooms as Rutland Water (2W-W) and Silversmith (2W-W).

M. J. Jefferson-Brown

Michael Jefferson-Brown, Whitbourne,

Hereford and Worcester, has done much to popularise the modern daffodils, particularly through his trade displays at the RHS Chelsea Show. Keeping blooms for this prestigious show has meant mastering the techniques for holding blooms back some four weeks beyond their normal flowering dates, but the efforts have benefited everyone. Breeding has been undertaken since 1944 and many fine novelties have been introduced including Hero (1O-R), which is probably the nearest as yet to the all-red trumpet daffodil. Whilst the quest for the perfect all-red flower has been a clear principal objective, in continuation of the work of W. O. Backhouse, other sub-divisions have been given some attention. It's True (1W-W), an enormous flower, and Tradition (1W-Y), are interesting cultivars that have been introduced.

F. C. Postles

As heir to John Lea's most recent seedlings, Clive Postles, based at Droitwich, Hereford and Worcester, is emerging as a serious contender for the highest accolades for raisers of new cultivars. Seed was produced in 1973 and having proved the techniques, recorded crosses, in the style of Lea, have been made since 1974 using the best commercial cultivars and unnamed seedlings. Already a frequent winner of the Bourne Cup (the Daffodil Society award for twelve cultivars raised by the exhibitor) Postles is aiming at the Engleheart Cup (the RHS equivalent award) and is building up stocks of some quite interesting cultivars. Recent introductions such as China Doll (2W-GWP) and Heslington (3W-GYR) have set a standard that is sure to be maintained in the future. Again, the use of the best available named cultivars and seedlings is being adopted as the route to new things, coupled with immaculate, full records of all crosses undertaken and attention to detail at all stages of cultivation.

Other English amateurs

There have been many very enthusiastic amateurs in England who have undertaken breeding work on a relatively small scale. Such is the unpredictability of the greater mechanics involved that even such small-scale activities have produced some notable cultivars that provide a spur to continue. Beauvallon (4Y-ORR) from David Lloyd and Cherrygardens (2W-GPP) from Noel Burr are typical examples. Others have continued to introduce named cultivars that have extended from such beginnings, usually with an increase in seeds sown, for example J. M. de Navarro and C. R. Wooton, who have both had a number of most impressive cultivars.

W. J. Dunlop

Within Northern Ireland there has been considerable activity in the development of daffodils. Much of the enthusiasm is traced directly, to Guy Wilson. However, until very recently Willie Dunlop, at Ballymena, was the figurehead of the daffodil breeders (and lovers) in the province. Many Dunlop cultivars have a refinement of form that makes them almost dateless and they have a quality of bulb that often is not given sufficient attention. The first breeding was undertaken in 1937 and throughout the first priority was clarity of colouring complemented by good texture. To me his most memorable cultivar is Newcastle (1W-Y) (Award of Merit, 1957) which, although registered thirty years ago, is still the outstanding flower of the sub-division and consistently rated within the top ten of all exhibition cultivars. Other Dunlop beauties that enhance his reputation are Down Patrick (1W-Y), of beautiful form if lacking in colour contrast, and Ballyrobert (1Y-Y), a magnificently formed and richly coloured trumpet.

T. Bloomer

Tom Bloomer, also based at Ballymena,

has made a considerable impact on the Northern Ireland scene as both raiser and an encourager of others. His total contribution is difficult to assess as cultivars are still to be released; however, by any standards it must be significant. The raising of seedlings commenced in 1950 following a number of successes as an exhibitor in London. Each year up to 1973 saw a number of crosses being attempted and a total of nearly 1,500 seeds were sown. Assessments are still being made on a number of stocks that will maintain the standards of the early successful introductions.

White trumpet daffodils are to many people associated with Bloomer's efforts and such beauties as White Star (1W-W), Silent Valley (1W-W) and Majestic Star (1W-W) give the lie to the idea that a white trumpet is just a white trumpet. Each of the three complements the others and each is an individual of great beauty. Yellow cultivars are perhaps typified by Golden Joy (2Y-Y) and Golden Jewel (2Y-Y); both have their enthusiasts and both take the highest honours. Many other sub-divisions have benefited from his work and Silent Cheer (3W-GYR) still stands as a wonderful introduction.

B. S. Duncan

Following closely on the work of Tom Bloomer is Brian Duncan of Omagh, Northern Ireland, who received early indoctrination from the masters. Whilst attending the RHS Show in 1964 some pollen was begged from Lionel Richardson and serious hybridisation has continued each year. Large numbers of crosses, sometimes with relatively high numbers of seeds, have been attempted, mostly with success. Attention has not been limited to Divisions 1, 2 and 3 and some breakthroughs have been made, notably in Divisions 4, 6 and 9. Many of the cultivars are relatively new to commerce but clearly some of them are destined to be successful on the show-bench and for garden decoration. Smokey Bear (4O-R) is the most highly coloured double currently available and in its season can be exceptionally beautiful. Vigilante (1W-W) is a distinctive white trumpet that has many loyal fans, whilst Doctor Hugh (3W-GOO) is destined to supplant the established favourites in its sub-division. Perhaps one of the most intriguing cultivars introduced has been Lilac Charm (6W-GPP) which is so typically cyclamineus in form and of such a delightful colour. There can be no doubt that even better things will be introduced from this enthusiastic source.

Other breeders in Northern Ireland

Maintaining the friendly rivalry within Northern Ireland are Sir Frank Harrison (Newtownards) and Kate Reade (Ballymena). Neither is overwhelmed by the Duncan cultivars, or their reputations, though they have not achieved quite the same show-bench successes. Sir Frank is quite meticulous in all of his breeding work and keen to have assessments on his newer seedlings from all quarters. His Capisco (3W-GYO) is always a beautiful sight. Golden Amber (2Y-Y) is an enchanting combination of pale amber and deep amber and of delightful form, whilst Kileen (2Y-O) has a wide orange bowl of a corona that is sunproof in most situations. Dove of Peace (6W-O) has been plagued with 'fly' but is a remarkably coloured cultivar. Kate Reade has many introductions to her credit. Her Gin and Lime (1Y-GWW), registered in 1973, has size, form and colouring to make it the outstanding reversed bicolour trumpet. Inniswood (1W-W) again shows that there is something about the province that encourages good white trumpets. Foundling (6W-P) is one of the most consistent cyclamineus hybrids of superb colouring but there appears to be some dubiety about its parentage.

J. Gerritsen

Over recent years breeding work in Holland has largely centred on novelties for garden decoration or floral art. The principal developer has been Jack Gerritsen whose hybridising has been largely for personal pleasure but has been responsible, against much criticism, for the vast range of 'split-corona' daffodils now available. The original work was with a white trumpet seedling which showed inconsistent splitting of the corona, and self-pollination was used to stabilise the form. These early crosses, from the 1920s, were gradually improved until the war years, but were kept together, and subsequently the new style was achieved. By much patience and selected outcrosses to cultivars with large cups the range of form and colours was gradually increased and improved. Jack Gerritsen has over one hundred registered cultivars to his credit of which some 75 per cent are split coronas (Division 11). Tiritomba (11Y-O) is a wonderful splash of colour, Sancerre (11W-Y) is of remarkably consistent form, King Size (11Y-Y) is a truly gigantic golden-yellow flower and Colorama (11Y-O) has a refinement of form that even appeals to some traditionalists. Most of the commercially popular split coronas have arisen from Jack Gerritsen's work but some of his other cultivars are also now popular. Little Gem (1Y-Y) is a delightful miniature of extremely good form and Baby Moon (7Y-Y) is a most pretty thing that does well in pots, the rock garden or window boxes.

Other Dutch hybridisers have played their part in the development of the daffodil. Most of their attention has been directed towards cultivars that have commercial attributes, such as earliness of flowering or intensity of colouring. Matthew Zandbergen received the Peter Barr Memorial Trophy in 1967 for a distinguished contribution to the development of daffodils both through his own hybridisation and the registration of cultivars of other raisers that were identified as commercial propositions. Some cultivars of Dutch origin are making their presence felt on the show-bench in the UK with varying success.

G. E. Mitsch

The leading American breeder of daffodils is Grant Mitsch, whose fifty years of endeavour have produced some extremely popular and successful cultivars from his plantings in Oregon. Mitsch's initial commercial interest in horticulture was with the gladiolus and having turned to the daffodil as a hobby in 1933 he began hybridising in 1934. A range of seedlings was produced and ultimately in 1945 daffodils replaced gladioli as the commercial enterprise. His initial success was with reversed bicolour trumpet daffodils by repeating a cross that had been attempted by Guy L. Wilson, but in large quantities (2,000-plus seeds), and resulted in Honeybird (1Y-W), still regarded as a good colour combination and form, Lunar Sea (1Y-W) and Nampa (1Y-W). Rima (1W-P), registered in 1954, is still one of the most brightly-coloured pink trumpets and is capable of competing at the highest level. A lot of attention has been given to reversed bicolours and Daydream (2Y-W), Chiloquin (1Y-W), Bethany (2W-Y) and Charter (2Y-W) are all consistent performers in a wide variety of situations and all derived from Binkie pollen on a reversed bicolour trumpet.

There has been significant attention to cultivars within Divisions 1, 2 and 3 and in particular to the pink-cupped cultivars, though not to the exclusion of any colour combination. Ruby Throat (2W-P) is still one of the most intensely-coloured cultivars and Audubon (3W-YYP) remains one of the exclusive group of pinks amongst the small-cupped cultivars. Aircastle (3W-Y), registered in 1958, is still popular in spite of its varying colour combinations. Cool Crystal (3W-GWW) (Award of Merit, 1985) remains consistent and, in spite of its inclination to hang its head, good for exhibition. More recent introductions include Lapine (3Y-YYO), a consistent rimmed cultivar, Pure Joy (3W-Y), a charming cultivar in a sadly neglected sub-division, and Queen Size (3W-Y). Grebe (4Y-YOO) and Spun Honey (4Y-Y) are remarkably consistent cultivars and whilst completely different are both charming doubles.

Grant Mitsch also directed attention to Divisions 5, 6, 7, 8 and 9, and by incorporating the relevant species into the breeding programmes has introduced some most attractive cultivars. Jet Fire (6Y-R) is one of the most reliable cyclamineus hybrids of wonderful colouring, Stratosphere (7Y-Y) is a refined and consistent clear yellow jonquil and Seraph (9W-GYR) a very pretty poeticus hybrid of circular form. Again, reversed bicolours have not been neglected and Dickcissel (7Y-W), from Binkie×N jonquilla, is one of the more colourful. There are still many interesting cultivars being assessed from Mitsch's extensive work and his daughters (Elise Havens and Eileen Frey) are likely to develop into new areas from the foundations so ably established by their devoted parents.

Dr T. D. Throckmorton

Dr Tom Throckmorton (Des Moines, Iowa) is typical of the enthusiastic amateur. He has taken the American Daffodil Society Data Bank through successive generations of computer technology and accumulated a vast record of the pedigrees of registered cultivars. This work has led to the useful publication *Daffodils to Show and Grow* and the revised system of daffodil classification based on colour coding, which is now in force. Dr Throckmorton has developed an intriguing range of toned cultivars that are almost impossible to slot into the coding. Experimental breeding commenced in the early 1960s after seeing the colour changes in Aircastle (registered as 3W-Y) and computer investigations of many pedigrees in a search for the genetic factor transmitting the toning. By expanding the programme to seek a wide range of luminous tones some delightful colour combinations have been achieved. These cultivars change colour as the blooms develop and create an interesting new dimension to show flowers, as well as some registration difficulties. Some fifty cultivars have been registered and whilst almost 50 per cent are yellow perianth examples of Division 3 it is the few toned cultivars that are outstanding. Of particular note are Suave (3Y-Y), Johnnie Walker (3Y-Y) and White Tie (3W-W), and no doubt others will be forthcoming.

M. W. Evans and other American breeders

Murray Evans (Oregon) has been responsible for an interesting range of cultivars following the registration of three cultivars in 1965. Replete (2Y-R), Descanso (1W-Y) and Sunapee (3Y-YYO) are consistent and of good form and there are many other cultivars across the major divisions. Murray Evans is clearly one of the foremost raisers in the USA and a consistent performer with his seedlings in the American Daffodil Society shows. Others who are maintaining the competition and helping the development of daffodils include Roberta Watrous, Bill Pannill and Willis Wheeler.

P. and G. Phillips

In any assessment of Australasian breeding work there are some names which inevitably emerge. New Zealander Phil Phillips (Otorahanga) is one of the better known and indeed was a tireless ambassador of the daffodil until his death in 1984. Phillips grew large quantities of bulbs and annually sowed large numbers of seedlings from humble beginnings in 1943. Many of the resultant new introductions did remarkably well on the show-bench and a number were registered, though not all. In his own right Phil Phillips registered about thirty-five cultivars of which Crimplene (3W-R), Trelay (3Y-O), Sedate (2W-P) and Bar None (1W-Y) are most widely available but Demand (2Y-Y) and Backchat (6Y-Y) are also good. In conjunction with his son, Graham, about fifty other cultivars have been registered and it is fortunate that the work is being continued. The vast majority of the cultivars were from Divisions 1, 2 and 3 though there was a smattering of good cyclamineus types.

D. S. Bell and other New Zealand breeders

Another successful and prolific New Zealand breeder is David Bell (Templeton). Most of his registrations are within the first three Divisions and are colourful forms. City Lights (2W-YYR) is a charming cultivar that has made a successful transfer to the northern hemisphere and has the style to be successful, and Stormy Weather (1W-Y) is now emerging as a useful bicolour trumpet. Mention must be made of the Brogdens, Jim O'More and Miss Mavis Verry: they have all produced some good cultivars and with the increasing exchanges between northern and southern hemispheres they are likely to have a greater influence upon the show scene.

W. J. and W. Jackson and other Australian breeders

Tasmania is an important source of many new daffodil cultivars. Much of the interest has stemmed from the work of three generations of the Jacksons who have introduced many successful cultivars from the initial work by William, Snr, in 1920. Important cultivars are Comal (1Y-Y) and Ristin (1Y-Y), which have brought a different, narrow trumpet into contention, and Cyros (1W-Y) which has become a useful addition to this very weak sub-division.

Perhaps the most consistent cultivar to come from Australia is Highfield Beauty (8Y-GYO), raised by H. R. Mott. It is generally acknowledged that only a small proportion of Australian cultivars are registered but none the less they make a significant contribution to the quest for something new and better. Again, many keen amateurs are finding better things to fill out those Divisions which are lacking in consistent cultivars, for example Harold Cross (Tasmania) with his Division 4 cultivars.

Rosewarne

In addition to the many individual breeders the Ministry of Agriculture have undertaken some interesting work at their Rosewarne Experimental Horticultural Station, Cornwall. The breeding work has concentrated upon the search for cultivars which will have importance in the cut flower trade, and hence has aimed to extend the flowering period and to produce cultivars that will cut well and have a good vase life. It is understood that work has also been directed to breeding cultivars which have improved and inbuilt resistance to the common daffodil diseases and it has been established that resistance to basal rot can be transmitted genetically. Many of the cultivars are only known by a number but occasionally one is named, eg Armynel (2Y-Y), prior to release as a commercial stock to the growers.

THE FUTURE

The search for improvements will never cease, but what will come next? From commercial interests new cultivars are required to meet the demands for cut flowers and so earlier cultivars will be a priority, provided they open well in water from the pencil-bud stage and have stems of a sufficient length. This is particularly important when cut flowers are to be exported to other EEC countries whose regulations need a stem length of some 12in (30cm). Flowering time is critical to commercial growers as the earlier blooms can be produced without forcing, hence a better financial return. Those whose prime consideration is the exhibition flower will be looking for clean colours in a better range, with the top priority still being given to the all-red flowers in any and all of the Divisions. Some attention may need to be directed to earlier-blooming exhibition cultivars to reverse recent trends. The garden decoration or dry bulb market will be looking for novelty of form and colour combination in addition to a good clean bulb that looks attractive. So there are many different objectives.

The novice breeder has plenty to go at and could initially concentrate upon colour combinations, such as a yellow and pink trumpet or the all-pink flower. Indeed, he or she may look at some of the neglected Divisions and try for a new combination of style and colour, perhaps to rival the multi-headed, split-corona Tripartite (11Y-Y), recently successfully introduced through the efforts of Richard Brooke, an enthusiastic amateur. Whatever the objective, it can provide an interesting extra dimension and the excuse for spending many hours during the long winter nights studying the parentage of the commercially-introduced cultivars and looking for possible leads towards something different.

Often one hears the comment that a particular bloom, as seen on the show-bench, is not an improvement upon an already registered cultivar. Assessment of the flower is only a very small part of the total evaluation of a seedling. The flower, the foliage and the bulb must all be subject to critical analysis and all are important. The ideal cultivar is still the one that gives every flower of show quality, is totally resistant to disease and reproduces itself rapidly with clean, solid bulbs: a lot of ideals that must find a place in the objectives of every breeder.

•9•

Choice of Cultivars

The official International Register of Daffodils now contains well in excess of 20,000 named cultivars, each having some distinguishing characteristic. Many of these registered cultivars have been lost to general cultivation. A number have historical importance as signposts of the developments which have taken place over the last fifty or so years, and perhaps some names have been registered but never allocated to a flower. A fairly large group is generally available through commercial sources or dispersals of specialist societies; others exist in such limited quantities that they cannot as yet be released into the world of commerce, even if they prove sufficiently attractive and robust for ultimate introduction. With so many named cultivars to choose from, where does one begin the quest for the right daffodil for particular circumstances?

However good the catalogue descriptions might be they can never adequately describe a particular cultivar and its potential uses. Descriptions supplemented by colour photographs can be of greater assistance but although some commercial organisations produce attractive catalogues they tend to give prominence to the well-established cultivars. There can be no substitute for looking at living blooms and this can be done at one or more of the spring shows, especially those with specialist classes for daffodils. At a show it is possible to assess the blooms and their appeal or potential for particular purposes or locations, though it must be recognised that most show-bench blooms have been rather cosseted and will only reproduce that sparkle when given similar treatment, though all are perfectly hardy garden subjects. The ideal way to assess cultivars is to see them growing, for preference in your own locality. Most growers are only too pleased to let others look and assess, and most of the specialist commercial growers have an open day when visitors are free to wander and look at the cultivars in growth. An alternative is to go and visit a keen amateur in your own locality, or tour a local botanical garden and see what they have got if your objective is more related to garden display or special effects.

The Royal Horticultural Society, through its Narcissus and Tulip Committee, has done much to assist with the problems associated with the selection of cultivars. The awards system for daffodils is split into three categories — exhibition, garden display and growth in pots or containers. The awards in the last two categories are only made after the cultivars have been grown in extensive 'trials' at the RHS Wisley Gardens under the careful ministrations of their qualified staff using bulbs of the selected cultivars supplied to them. The awards for exhibition are made when a grower supplies the defined number of blooms for assessment as cut flowers at one of the Society's shows at Vincent Square in London, when they can be inspected by the members of the Narcissus and Tulip Committee.

The highest level of award is the First Class Certificate (FCC) in each of the three categories and this usually implies that the cultivar is considered to be eminently suitable for the defined use or uses. Potentially good cultivars for a particular purpose, which may need further assessment in later years, can be given an Award of Merit (AM). Some cultivars on their first presentation to the Narcissus and Tulip Committee may be sufficiently notable to receive either a Preliminary Certificate of Commendation (PCC), usually limited to exhibition cultivars, or a Highly Commended (HC) which is usually applicable in the case of blooms for garden display or for pots. Very often in catalogue descriptions one will see FCC mentioned for a cultivar, which indeed will have received such an award, but it could be for one, two or three of the defined categories and so a little additional research may be necessary. A cultivar with an FCC for exhibition may not have the form or constitution to do well in a garden in competition with other plants or shrubs, and likewise an FCC for garden display does not indicate that the cultivar has the potential to be successful on the show-bench or respond to typical pot-growing techniques.

Naturally, some cultivars have the constitution and form to receive an FCC for different purposes and therefore have that much more value to the grower. Some people have the idea that the higher the price the better will be the cultivar and the more it will enhance a show collection or a garden display. With some of the more recent introductions it may be true that the high price reflects the breeder's assessment of the cultivar's potential, or perhaps its likely use in a further breeding programme. However, with some of the generally available cultivars the price may be no more than a reflection of the amount of stock held by the supplier.

The following sections give details of cultivars which have values for defined purposes. To some extent the listings inevitably reflect my personal preferences; however, these assessments have been made over many years and from seeing the different cultivars in growth.

MULTI-PURPOSE CULTIVARS

These cultivars have been selected as they have proved over the years to be reliable for pot cultivation, both for exhibition and decorative effect, for garden display and for the production of specimen exhibition blooms. They are now readily available and can be used in show classes with relatively low price limits or in classes where three, five or seven blooms of a cultivar are required. Most will produce the exceptional bloom that could take a Best in Show award and yet are durable and appealing in the garden.

Kingscourt (1Y-Y) Registered in 1938, this cultivar has three FCCs. It is a true trumpet daffodil of glowing deep yellow. Not every bloom is of exhibition quality but some super ones are produced in most seasons. This short, sturdy grower looks well in a pot for display and is not too tall to be damaged by winds when planted in the garden. With reasonable attention it multiplies well.

Saint Keverne (2Y-Y) Registered many years ago (1949) and is the holder of three FCCs. By measurement the blooms are Division 2 but they have the appearance of a trumpet daffodil. The blooms are produced very freely but they do not have the size or form of Kingscourt, being more distinctively starry. It is a relatively tall grower and when in pots needs to be kept very cool if the stems are not to overbalance and spoil the display. In the garden its height makes it more suitable for the rear of a border than an exposed planting in grass but its rate of increase and ability to produce good blooms make it an invaluable investment. It is becoming a popular cut flower now that sufficient stocks are available and has the constitution to last well in water when cut in the bud. As a parent it is proving useful for passing a degree of resistance to basal rot to its progeny.

Merlin (3W-YYR) Another holder of three FCCs which has been around since 1956. Its petals are remarkably white and an individual bloom can be quite arresting, whilst a dozen in a pot are breathtaking. It is perhaps a little long in the stem for some pot work or garden display but the impact which is made more than offsets this apparent difficulty. Perhaps its major fault is that the red rim of the corona is not entirely sun-proof and whilst from a distance the blooms look impressive, at close quarters they lack the perfection of detail in the corona. It is a reliable exhibition cultivar even if the colouring of the corona is not always consistently distributed in even whorls.

Dove Wings (6W-Y) A splendid cyclamineus hybrid registered in 1949 and a most consistent performer in the majority of situations. It is a relatively short grower, about 12in (30cm), and produces a number of secondary growths which enhance the display and extend its life. On first opening the perianth is creamy coloured but as it becomes fully reflexed it develops to a pure white. The nodding, graceful heads are quite durable though the yellow in the corona does fade slightly as the flower ages. A truly all-round flower that has had a wide range of awards.

Daydream (2Y-W) To the amazement of many people this cultivar was raised in the United States of America. It is perhaps the most durable cultivar from the work of Grant Mitsch and was registered in 1960. It produces some impressive blooms for the show-bench. When its true colouring is achieved — the sparkling white corona is set off by its fine yellow rim and the golden perianth — it is most appealing. Being a sturdy, short-growing cultivar, about 15in (38cm), it is ideally suited to cultivation in pots for home decoration and for garden display. Price fluctuates very much but due to its popularity it is becoming available in greater numbers.

141

THREE CULTIVARS that are consistent performers on the show-bench but also make impressive displays in the home and garden. (Top) Merlin (3W-YYR); (bottom left) Rainbow (2W-WWP); (bottom right) April Love (1W-W). The three blooms were a first prize exhibit at the Harrogate Spring Show (1986) in the class requiring one bloom each from Divisions 1, 2 and 3

Tête-à-Tête (6Y-O) A cultivar that will always have a success or two on the show-bench but will never achieve an FCC for exhibition. However, it has a wide range of awards, including an FCC for garden display. Classed as a short-growing cultivar it continues to extend its stem as the flowers develop so that even when the flowers are first opening at a height of 6in (15cm) the final stem may be 12in (30cm). Usually each main stem with its two heads of true cyclamineus form is surrounded by secondary growths which may be double-headed though frequently they have only a single head. In pots it makes an impressive decorative display which can last for three to four weeks. In the rock garden or naturalised in grass it produces a compact and intense display of colour.

Passionale (2W-P) Not in the same awards league as Kingscourt, though it has received at least an AM for each of the three categories. Registered in 1956, this is arguably the most versatile pink cultivar currently available in large quantities. The pink colouring may not be sufficiently intense to please everyone yet it is clear and distinctly recognisable as a true pink. It is a robust grower that does well in pots and does not grow too tall to lose balance; it also shapes up well when growing in grass.

There are many other cultivars which may be considered as multi-purpose but they are perhaps usually associated with a specialist use. The listing may change over the years as other cultivars become more readily available and more widely recognised. However, the seven named above give a true representation of all that is good in multi-purpose cultivars.

HOME DECORATION IN POTS AND CONTAINERS

There are many cultivars which give super displays when grown specifically for home decoration but which do not, in other situations, always give of their best.

Nylon (12W-W) A charming bulbocodium hybrid that is a dwarf grower and looks splendid in a small pot. With only a little manipulation of conditions it can be in flower for Christmas Day as a focus of attention.

Paperwhite Grandiflora (8W-W) By the use of treated bulbs very early flowers can be obtained. It is ideal for growing in containers using pebbles and water only and does not need a period of darkness, so can be watched through all stages of growth. Its memorable and characteristic perfume will pervade the whole room. This cultivar is best treated as a disposable bulb once used in pots or containers. To grow successfully in other situations it needs protection and a good summer baking.

Charity May (6Y-Y) Almost interchangeable with Dove Wings but because of its intense yellow colouring is more readily perceived as a typical daffodil and therefore that much more welcome when growing in a pot. It is a short grower and can be seen as a whole with its pot or container. This long-lasting flower gives a very good return on the outlay and is becoming more readily available.

Minnow (8W-Y) A delightful shortgrowing cultivar — 8in (20cm) — that can rightly be classed as a miniature. The main stem from each bulb can have four or five dainty heads; subsidiary stems are produced in great numbers and may have two or three heads only. However, a great number of flower-heads are produced to give an impressive display. It is now readily available as commercial growers have found areas which offer ideal growing conditions compatible with good rate of increase and large-sized bulbs.

Geranium (8W-O) As with most tazettas the flowers are initially produced on short, sturdy stems which elongate as the opened flowers develop to their peak. The perianth is pure white, usually with a few creases and folds though these do not detract from the impression of the whole. The short, vivid orange coronas give a richness of colouring to the total head of flowers. Stems can carry four to six florets so that in a small space a lot of colour can be achieved. An interesting perfume adds to its appeal.

Spellbinder (1Y-W) A true trumpet daffodil that opens a uniform sulphur yellow. As the flower ages the trumpet colouring fades to almost white, especially in the centre of the corona, to create a very interesting effect. The perianth is rather narrow by modern standards but the contrast of colouring makes the whole bloom impressive. A fairly strong grower, about 16in (40cm), it really needs cool growing conditions.

Rainbow (2W-WWP) A super flower for an impressive focal point in a room or display. The perianth has great substance and creamy whiteness to display the broad rim of pink which edges the corona. The pink is tinged with orange and is variable in colouring dependent upon the growing conditions, but nevertheless is quite arresting. The foliage is upright and the stems are about 17in (42cm) tall.

Erlicheer (4W-W) Although registered as a double daffodil this is really a double form of tazetta which retains a characteristic and pervading perfume. The two or three heads per stem are heavily doubled blooms of a delightful creamy white. Foliage is deep green and robust, and serves as a good foil for the blooms.

Though this is still quite scarce, to my mind it is a much better proposition in pots than either Cheerfulness (4W-Y) or its yellow sport.

Arctic Gold (1Y-Y) Chosen against the wide range of trumpet daffodils that are generally favoured for pot cultivation as it has a much neater form and purer yellow colouring. It grows fairly tall, about 18in (44cm). The flowers are not excessively large but with the broad overlapping perianths they do not appear out of proportion to the height.

Galway (2Y-Y) Not a cultivar noted for its perfection of form but still quite capable of producing some very neat blooms. The good clear yellow and a fairly long corona can give the impression of a trumpet daffodil. It has a very strong constitution and is a sturdy grower.

FOR FLORAL DISPLAYS AS CUT BLOOMS

Every cultivar can be made into an attractive floral arrangement, some more easily than others. There are some cultivars which I find very interesting for floral displays and would grow them specifically for that purpose.

Honeybird (1Y-W) A pale lemon, full-trumpet daffodil that has an attractive twist to the inner three perianth segments. As the flower ages the colouring of the trumpet fades to near white with a deeper colouring at the rim.

Cassata (11W-W) An intriguing split-corona daffodil that produces flat double discs from perianth and corona. It lacks colour to be impressive on its own but with different textures and shadings of foliage it can be attractive for a floral display.

Dickcissel (7W-Y) Carries two or three flower-heads per stem and has the style of a true jonquilla. As the flowers age to maturity the shallow cups turn almost pure white and there is a halo of the same colour on the perianth. The corona and halo are highlighted by the clear yellow of the remainder of the perianth. This very durable cultivar gives life to a display as the individual flower-heads develop to maturity at slightly different times.

Sancerre (11W-Y) A more refined split corona daffodil having a delicately yellow corona offset by the white perianth. A substantial and long lasting cultivar.

144

FOR SHOWING AS CUT BLOOMS

Selection of cultivars for showing is a difficult proposition as so much depends upon the money available and upon the level of competition being attempted. Styles do change with the passage of time and as newer cultivars become readily available, and this means that assessments have to be regularly updated.

The established favourites, which would be a reliable collection for beginners, are:

Viking (1Y-Y) A refined yellow trumpet that prefers cultivation in the open ground but can be persuaded to produce good blooms from pots.

Empress of Ireland (1W-W) Of immense size, this white trumpet is a very consistent performer but for pure whiteness needs protection and preferably growing in a pot.

Drumboe (2W-P) A very delicate but true pink that does well at all levels of competition. Occasionally the perianth appears to lack substance but retains its most impressive form. The major problem is the variation of the colouring and the proportion of the corona that is definably pink.

Newcastle (1W-Y) A very consistent bicolour trumpet that does well in most situations but needs pot cultivation to get the best degree of whiteness into the perianth. The perianth tends to hood over the trumpet but it is most amenable to dressing for the show-bench.

Unique (4W-Y) A charming and consistent double that moved from relative obscurity to show-bench favourite in a very short time. As with most doubles it loses some fullness of inner petaloids if the bulbs are small but it has an immaculate perianth that is a perfect foil for the bloom. Again in common with many doubles, it is prone to 'green back' (green

discoloration of the back of the perianth) in cold damp seasons.

Avenger (2W-R) A remarkable cultivar that has a beautiful round perianth and an intensely-coloured corona. It is unfortunate that the edge of the corona is inclined to burn in bright sunlight but the form is attractive and balanced. There is some staining of colour into the perianth which enhances the appeal of the bloom. I have chosen this in preference to Rockall (3W-R) which is a larger yet refined cultivar that appears to respond well in only some areas.

Golden Aura (2Y-Y) A most consistent performer with a delightful bowl-shaped corona. It is a very neat flower that regularly produces blooms of refinement, though if grown to a large size it may be less consistent. In many ways it sets the standard for an all-yellow large-cup daffodil.

Shining Light (2Y-ORR) A truly reliable cultivar that has an appealing faint orange flush to the perianth. By modern standards the perianth may be too starry and lack overlap but it always makes an impact.

Verona (3W-W) Still a regular first prize winner and of good form. It takes the flowers a little time to achieve an acceptable level of overall whiteness but the whole bloom is balanced and well held on the stem.

Broomhill (2W-W) Often underestimated as a show cultivar but it produces blooms of substance and of quite sparkling colouring. As with many of the relatively old cultivars (it was registered in 1965) it lacks some overlap in the perianth but it is a distinctive cultivar.

The cultivars for use at the highest level of competition include:

Ballyrobert (1Y-Y) Not a new cultivar but one that is still quite scarce. It has good seasons and less good ones but has a reliability in colouring and form.

Dailmanach (2W-P) Probably the most consistent cultivar available and capable of producing impressive and immaculate blooms in most conditions. The colouring does vary according to the cultural conditions but it is always distinctive and obviously acceptable as a true pink. Although clearly a Division 2 by measurement it looks like a true trumpet daffodil. It is also very useful for breeding pinks.

Purbeck (3W-YYO) A truly delightful rimmed cultivar that has a most impressive sheen to the perianth. The orange colouring is very clear but can vary in its proportions along the corona, though always distinctive in collections.

Doctor Hugh (2W-GOO) Perhaps the best of the modern generation of intensely-coloured Division 3 cultivars. The colouring of the corona is heightened by the green eye and is almost sunproof in most conditions. The perianth is a clear white and is not stained by colour running from the corona. It has the ability to produce blooms of impressive size and refinement.

Grand Prospect (2Y-W) When fully reversed, which takes about seven days from bud burst, it has a most enchanting colouring. The perianth has good form and colour, and the corona is clearly Division 2. The tendency is to cut the blooms too early but they need time on the plant to develop their true colouring. This cultivar is still fairly scarce though it does produce remarkably good bulbs.

Brierglass (2W-W) Created quite a sensation when shown as a seedling due to its great similarity of form to Golden Aura — in fact it is still regarded as an all-white version of that reliable cultivar. From show-bench successes it would appear to have great potential based on consistency and significant substance. In growth it always looks healthy.

Gay Kybo (4W-O) A remarkable double daffodil which is always symmetrical from outer perianth to the centre of the bloom. The perianth tends to hood the bloom but it can, with care, be dressed smooth. The colouring does not appeal to everyone as the degree of whiteness lacks sparkle but the orange petaloids are quite distinctive.

Achduart (3Y-R) Since its registration in 1972 this cultivar has set the standard for this particular sub-division. It is remarkably consistent and if any fault is to be acknowledged it must be that the perianth colouring is a shade too pale. In all other respects this cultivar is essential for collection classes as well as being reliable as a single bloom.

April Love (1W-W) For a number of years this cultivar failed to live up to its original promise. However, it now appears to have settled down to its different environments and is consistently producing large blooms of impressive form. Not everyone's idea of a trumpet daffodil, but it is distinctive and full of substance, and a break from the flat double-triangle perianth which is so popular.

Loch Rimsdale (2Y-R) Always attracts attention due to the flush of orange colouring in the perianth. A beautiful round flower that is most consistent and a strong grower, though it may take some time for it to stabilise in different parts of the country.

In addition, there are many other relatively new, or expensive, cultivars which have their supporters and which are worthy of brief comment:

Lapine (3Y-YYO) Potentially an important rimmed Division 3.

Gin and Lime (1Y-GWW) A reversed bicolour trumpet of impeccable form.

Sabine Hay (3O-R) The most intensely-coloured cultivar but of weak poise.

Ferndown (3Y-Y) Perhaps the best yellow colouring in this sub-division.

Smokey Bear (4O-R) A super double of very nice colouring.

Gold Convention (1Y-Y) Perceived as a true all-yellow trumpet of very rich colouring.

White Star (1W-W) Impeccable petal lay and of classic form but rigid in the neck in some conditions.

Stormy Weather (1W-Y) Settling down as a splendid bicolour of distinctive colour.

White Convention (1W-W) Potentially as indispensable as Gold Convention.

Most of the cultivars identified have come from Divisions 1 to 4, and indeed these are given priority in most show schedules. However, the other Divisions should not be forgotten even if there is a shortage of good reliable cultivars for use on the show-bench. Some useful subjects are:

Arish Mell (5W-W) Of typical triandus form; with three blooms per stem it is quite stunning, with four it is breathtaking.

Tuesday's Child (5W-Y) The most consistent cultivar with this colour combination. Still quite scarce but invaluable for collections and can be grown to good size.

Golden Wings (6Y-Y) Not quite sufficiently reflexed in the perianth to be universally acceptable as a cyclamineus hybrid, but is extremely useful as it flowers much later than the majority of cultivars in the Division and is a true golden colour.

Elizabeth Ann (6W-GWP) A truly delightful form and with the delicate rim to the shallow corona makes a most impressive sight.

Stratosphere (7Y-Y) Typical jonquil form and a delightful clear colouring. It can attain a good size and maintain uniformity through its three flower-heads.

Highfield Beauty (8Y-GYO) Usually only three quite large heads per stem and a delightful orange rim to the coronas. It does burn in bright sunlight but can be persuaded to maintain its colouring.

Avalanche (8W-Y) Very often carries twenty flower-heads per stem and has a refinement in the perianth not usually associated with the tazettas. Has a good reputation but needs careful attention if it is to be persuaded to remain floriferous over a number of seasons.

147

FOR THE ROCKERY AND TROUGHS

It is inevitable that we need to look at the smaller types and especially the species. Although they are generally regarded as difficult subjects they can do extremely well if a little extra attention is given to provide conditions which are not too different from those normally available. Some attractive subjects are:

N triandus albus (10W-W) Often referred to as Angel's Tears, this is a charming plant that needs a well-drained pocket in the rockery and must get full summer sun to bake the bulbs ready to give of their best the following season.

N rupicola (10Y-Y) There are a number of different clones of this vivid yellow species. They do not like being disturbed but once established make a wonderful mid-season splash of colour. They are not too particular about conditions but not too happy when in competition with surface-rooting plants.

N juncifolius (10Y-Y) More correctly *N requienii* — a delightful species growing to some 6in (15cm) with perfectly-formed perianth and shallow corona. Must have good drainage and be able to dry out fully in the summer months.

N watieri (10W-W) Similar in style and size to *N juncifolius* but of a quite amazing whiteness. It needs to be given close attention and will usually benefit from some protection if the flowers are to be encouraged to give of their best. Only increases slowly by bulb division.

N cyclamineus (10Y-Y) With its narrow trumpet and sharply-reflexed perianth this species does not appeal to everyone yet its vivid yellow colouring makes an instant impact. It prefers a slightly acid condition and likes a degree of dampness in the ground at most times. It will quickly establish itself and if in favourable conditions usually sets seed.

Hawera (5Y-Y) A shallow-cupped triandus hybrid that produces some four to seven heads per stem. It usually comes into flower quite late in the season and is a very durable bloom. It is not too particular about location but does need a fairly rich soil to sustain the bulbs which divide quite rapidly.

Segovia (3W-Y) A true miniature version of a small-cupped daffodil. The glistening white perianth slightly reflexes at the tips and acts as a perfect foil for the delicate clear-yellow corona. A quite sturdy plant, but some support may be necessary for the flowers which can cause the stems to bend, especially when weighed down with rain on the petals.

Pencrebar (4Y-Y) A wonderful all-yellow double that is reminiscent of a

GOOD STAGING OF BLOOMS is essential for successful exhibition. Four entries for the Webb Trophy (Daffodil Society Show 1986) were differentiated by the overall presentation of each set of three vases. The cultivars used by the exhibitors were (*left to right*) Banbridge (1Y-Y), Ceylon (2Y-O), Saint Keverne (2Y-Y); Shining Light (2Y-ORR), Rainbow (2W-WWP), Merlin (3W-GYR) (First Award); Newcastle (1W-Y) Shining Light (2Y-ORR), Woodland Star (3W-R) (Third); Drumboe (2W-P), Daydream (2Y-W), Aircastle (3W-Y) (Second)

The Webb Trophy

Three Cultivars from not
less than two Divisions,
three stems of each.

A TYPICAL TRADE DISPLAY at Harrogate Spring Show, which provides an ideal opportunity to study the different types of daffodil. This display is predominantly of miniatures and smaller growing types — ideal subjects for rockeries and small gardens

MISTY GLEN (2W-GWW) an outstanding cultivar with the green colouring in the base of the corona giving an interesting depth to the bloom

PASSIONALE (2W-P) is probably the most widely grown pink daffodil. Raised by Guy L. Wilson in Northern Ireland, it was registered in 1956 by F. E. Board. Each year it receives many awards for exhibitions and does extremely well in borders and mass plantings

SEGOVIA (3W-Y) one of the dainty cultivars raised by Alec Gray. It looks superb in the rockery or in small pots, and creates pretty arrangements for use as table centrepieces or on the dressing-table

camellia bloom. It is capable of producing two heads per stem when cultivation is good, though most of the off-sets are likely to produce single heads. The flower is beautiful but in a wet season the heads hold a lot of water and become bowed down. It is better planted in a very sheltered spot where it can be well watered in spring and early summer so that the blooms can be fully appreciated.

Clare (7Y-Y) Makes a wonderful strong plant with the greenish-yellow blooms held erectly above the foliage. As with most jonquilla hybrids, it needs to dry out properly in the summer months and then will multiply fairly rapidly.

Xit (3W-W) The most brilliantly white hybrid miniature daffodil with a perfec-

tion of form that is instantly appealing. It is still quite scarce though it does respond well to good cultivation.

There are many other cultivars that come to mind as splendid subjects for the rock garden. Many of the cyclamineus hybrids are particularly attractive, especially:

Jet Fire (6Y-R) Very richly coloured and a very early-flowering cultivar. It produces a fair number of secondary growths to prolong the flowering period.

Foundling (6W-P) Not sufficiently reflexed to satisfy some purists but nevertheless a splendid strong-growing cultivar that attracts attention with its vivid pink cup.

AN ATTRACTIVE SPRING-FLOWER ARRANGEMENT. This style is reminiscent of the earliest representations of identfiable daffodils, in Dutch paintings

Lilac Charm (6W-GPP) Of classic form with a delightful apple-blossom pink corona that has an attractive roll to its rim. It is still quite scarce but always creates much interest.

Other types are available and fortunately the interest in the smaller species and cultivars appears to be encouraging commercial concerns to attempt to propagate the best of those available so that they can be introduced to a wider audience. Some attractive examples are:

Sun Disc (7Y-Y) A charming jonquilla that is an intriguing shade of yellow.

W. P. Milner (1W-W) A trumpet style with a ragged perianth, but long lasting.

Little Gem (1Y-Y) A perfect yellow trumpet that grows to not more than 8in (20cm) and stands well in most conditions.

Rarer subjects are available almost as an investment for the future. Not all of them are easy to grow. They are all interesting and, after the efforts involved to get them established, can do well. Examples are:

N eystettensis (10Y-Y) A historical favourite which has been known by a range of names (including Queen Anne's Double Jonquil). Very slow to multiply but can be propagated from seed.

Pequenita (7Y-Y) A vivid golden-yellow jonquil that is outstandingly beautiful.

Little Sentry (7Y-Y) A very sturdy jonquil that responds quite well when grown in full sun.

FOR MASS PLANTING

Top of my list for mass planting come the Tenby daffodils (*N obvallaris*) and the Lent lily (*N pseudonarcissus*). Neither is of outstanding form but they evoke so many memories of daffodils growing in remote areas of the Lake District that they give much pleasure. To these should be added Van Sion, the old golden-yellow double that has a constitution of iron and will thrive in most situations.

Most large-scale plantings naturally use the less expensive cultivars which are readily available in quantity. Ice Follies (2W-W), Semper Avanti (2W-O) and Mount Hood (1W-W) give good displays, as do many of the yellow trumpets that are affectionately, if incorrectly, known as King Alfred. Groupings of single cultivars are preferable to mixed plantings, especially where some may be of doubtful origins and unsuited to the competition usually encountered in mass plantings. In addition to the multi-purpose cultivars described earlier, useful subjects are:

February Gold (6Y-Y) A free-flowering early cyclamineus type that gives a good account of itself usually early in spring.

Court Martial (2Y-R) A wonderfully-coloured cultivar that produces masses of solid flowers.

Vigil (1W-W) A fairly refined white trumpet that appears to stand the vagaries of a normal spring very well.

Liberty Bells (5Y-Y) With two or three delicate nodding heads per stem it creates quite an impact and is long lasting.

Sweetness (7Y-Y) A quite refined jonquil that has the characteristic scent, is long lasting and produces a good quantity of blooms.

Loch Owskeich (2Y-O) Another good-coloured cultivar that stands the different weather conditions quite well in spite of its size and length of stem.

Brabazon (1Y-Y) Comes into bloom quite early and has large well-coloured flowers that match most people's idea of a 'proper' daffodil.

It is always worth experimenting with different cultivars to see how they perform with you. Inevitably, some will not like the way you treat them and others will become rampant. Most suppliers price the newer or less common cultivars in units of one, three or five bulbs. Even one bulb of a cultivar which does like your conditions will multiply and in a period as short as five years will make an interesting clump of five to eight, or more, blooms of something a little different and of great pleasure.

THE LENT LILY (*N pseuodonarcissus*) is a wild daffodil found naturalised in many parts of the UK. It makes a charming display when growing in grass. Uprooting Lent lilies from their natural habitats should not be attempted, they can be obtained from commercial sources

USEFUL CULTIVARS

Over a period of many years every grower of daffodils will try a wide range of cultivars. Some will acclimatise, some will not be happy in the particular conditions. The following is a limited range of cultivars that have proved useful in effecting a comprehensive display of daffodils. The cultivar name is followed by:

a) Colour coding in brackets, eg (4W-R)
b) Flowering season
   1=very early season   3=mid to main season   5=late season
   2=early season   4=main season   6=early summer
c) Height
   (1)=recognised miniature   (3)=a plant up to 20in (50cm)
   (2)=a plant generally up to 15in (38cm)   (4)=a plant over 20in (50cm)
d) Indication of significant perfume, P
e) Ability to produce show-quality blooms
   S=occasionally   SS=fairly frequently
f) Awards after trial at Wisley
   (AM)=award of Merit   (FCC)=First Class Certificate

Acropolis (4W-R), 4, (4), SS.
Actea (9W-GYR), 4, (4), P, (FCC).
Air Marshal (2Y-R), 4, (4), S, (AM).
Aircastle (3W-Y), 5, (4), SS. Colour varies through growing season.
Altruist (3O-R), 5, (3), S.
Amber Castle (2Y-WPP), 4, (3), S. Pink colouring can be very faint.
Ambergate (2O-R), 5, (4).
Andalusia (6Y-YRR), 1, (2).
Aosta (2W-P), 2, (3), S.
April Tears (5Y-Y), 6, (1). Very similar in form to Hawera.
Arbar (2W-O), 3, (4).
Arctic Doric (2W-W), 2, (3), (AM). Very startling whiteness and a strong grower.
Arctic Flame (2W-YOO), 3, (3).
Argosy (1Y-Y), 4, (3).
Ariel (3W-OOY), 4, (3), S. A most attractive yellow rim to the corona.
Arkle (1Y-Y), 2, (4), SS. Produces some very large blooms.
Armada (2Y-O), 2, (4), (FCC). Clear colouring.

Armagh (1Y-Y), 3, (4), S.
N asturiensis (10Y-Y), 1, (1). Ideal for rockeries. Gives very early colour.
Audubon (3W-YYP), 4, (3), S.
Aurum (1Y-Y), 3, (3), S.
Avalon (2Y-W), 3, (3), S. A very sturdy plant.
Ave (2W-W), 3, (3), S.
Avenger (2W-R), 4, (3), S.
N bulbocodium conspicuus (10Y-Y), 1, (1). A variable species that gives good highlights in a rockery.
Baby Moon (7Y-Y), 6, (1).
Balalaika (2Y-YYR), 2, (3).
Ballygarvey (1W-Y), 4, (3), (AM). Has a very good colour contrast.
Balvenie (2W-GPP), 5, (3), SS. In some conditions has a very defined rim to corona.
Banbridge (1Y-Y), 2, (3), S. A strong consistent grower.
Bayard (1Y-Y), 4, (3), S, (AM).
Bebop (7W-Y), 6, (1), P.
Beersheba (1W-W), 2, (3). A very large flower of good form.

Ben Hee (2W-W), 3, (3), SS. A flower of good substance.

Benvoy (3W-GWW), 4, (3), S.

Bere Ferrers (4W-O), 4, (3), SS.

Beryl (6Y-O), 3, (2).

Bethany (2Y-W), 3, (3), S. Reverses well and is a sturdy plant.

Binkie (2Y-W), 4 (3).

Birdalone (2W-GWW), 3, (3), S.

Bittern (12Y-O), 3, (2). Not a strong colour contrast but a good plant.

Blarney (3W-OOY), 4, (4).

Bobbysoxer (7Y-YYO), 4, (1), S.

Border Flame (2Y-R), 3, (3).

Borrobol (2W-R), 3, (3), SS.

Brahms (2W-ORR), 4, (3).

Bramley (2W-P), 2, (3). A distinct shade of pink.

Bravoure (1W-Y), 3, (4), SS, (AM).

Bridesmaid (2W-WPP), 4, (4). Strong plant with nice colouring.

Brookfield (2W-W), 2, (3), S.

Broughshane (1W-W), 4, (4). A powerful plant but now superseded for show work.

Bunclody (2Y-R), 4, (3).

Buncrana (2W-O), 3, (3).

Butterscotch (2Y-Y), 3, (3). Impressive colour and size.

Cairn Toul (3W-ORR), 4, (3), SS.

Cairngorm (2Y-W), 3, (3). Similar to Amber Castle.

Camelot (2Y-Y), 3, (3), S. A very strong plant.

Canary (7YW-W), 5, (3). Reverses well and has a distinct halo around the corona.

Canasta (11W-Y), 2, (4). Corona fades to whitish as the flowers age.

Cantabile (9W-GGR), 6, (3), P, S. Colour burns in sunlight but impressive whiteness to corona.

Carbineer (2Y-O), 4, (4).

Carlton (2Y-Y), 2, (4). Very reliable in all conditions.

Carnmoon (3W-GWY), 4, (3).

Cassata (11W-W), 3, (3).

Ceylon (2Y-O), 2, (3), (FCC).

Charter (2Y-W), 3, (4), (AM).

Cheerfulness (4W-Y), 5, (3), P. An interesting multi-headed double, strong grower.

Chiloquin (1Y-W), 4, (3), S. Good plant but flowers are quite small.

Chinese White (3W-GWW), 5, (3). Strong plant but flowers are quite grey by comparison with recent introductions.

Chungking (3Y-R), 3, (3).

Clare (7Y-Y), 5, (1), P, S.

Cloud Nine (2Y-W), 4, (3). Could almost be classified as an intermediate, reverses well.

Clumber (3W-Y), 5, (3), S. A robust very round flower with very short cup.

Cool Contrast (1W-Y), 3, (3).

Cool Crystal (3W-GWW), 5, (4), S. Hangs its head but very strong plant.

Coral Ribbon (2W-YYP), 3, (3).

Cristobal (1W-Y), 4, (3), S.

Danes Balk (2W-W), 4, (3).

Debutante (2W-P), 3, (3).

Delightful (3W-GYY), 3, (3).

Desdemona (2W-W), 3, (3). Strong grower.

Dolly Mollinger (11W-OWO), 4, (3), S.

Don Carlos (2W-R), 4, (4), S. Corona burns but still looks radiant.

Double Event (4W-Y), 4, (4), S, (FCC).

Doubtful (3Y-O), 2, (3), S.

Downpatrick (1W-Y), 3, (5), S. Not a strong colour contrast but impressive plant.

Dream Castle (3W-W), 5, (3). Strong plant that needs plenty of space.

Dulcie Joan (2W-WWP), 4, (3).

Early Mist (2W-W), 2, (4). Gives the impression of being a trumpet; consistent performer.

Easter Moon (2W-GWW), 3, (4), S. A very reliable cultivar.

Eddy Canzony (2W-YYO), 3, (3).

Egg Nogg (4W-Y), 5, (3).

Emily (2Y-Y), 4, (3).

Estremadura (2Y-O), 3, (3), SS.

a) Colour coding in brackets,
   eg (4W-R)
b) Flowering season
   1 = very early season
   2 = early season
   3 = mid to main season
   4 = main season
   5 = late season
   6 = early summer
c) Height
   (1) = recognised miniature
   (2) = a plant generally up to 15in
         (38cm)
   (3) = a plant up to 20in (50cm)
   (4) = a plant over 20in (50cm)
d) Indication of significant perfume, P
e) Ability to produce show-quality
   blooms
   S = occasionally
   SS = fairly frequently
f) Awards after trial at Wisley
   (AM) = award of Merit
   (FCC) = First Class Certificate

Evenlode (2W-WWY), 4, (3).

N eystettensis (10Y-Y), 2, (1). Also
quoted as Queen Anne's double
daffodil.

Falaise (4W-O), 6, (4).

Fiji (4Y-Y), 3, (3), S.

Fire Island (2Y-O), 3, (3).

Form Master (1W-Y), 3, (3).

Fortune (2Y-O), 2, (4), (FCC). Good
strong grower.

Gay Challenger (4W-R), 4, (3), S.
Large-sized flower that is consistent.

Gay Song (4W-W), 4, (3). Very large
blooms on strong plants.

Gay Time (4W-R), 4, (3).

Glacier (1W-W), 3, (2), (AM). Very
large blooms on strong stems.

Gold Frills (3W-WWY), 5, (3).

Gold Phantom (1Y-Y), 3, (3).

Golden Amber (2Y-ORR), 3, (3), S.
Strong grower of quite delicate
colour.

Golden Ducat (4Y-Y), 2, (4). A
consistent performer that creates a
good display of colour.

Golden Harvest (1Y-Y), 1, (3).

Golden Jewel (2Y-GYY), 3, (3), SS.

Golden Rapture (1Y-Y), 3, (3), S. A
good plant.

Golden Sovereign (1Y-Y), 3, (3), S.
Very similar to Golden Rapture and
a good grower.

Grand Monarque (8W-Y), 4, (3), P.
Needs a good summer baking,
produces solid bulbs.

Grand Soleil D'Or (8Y-O), 1, (2), P.
Bulbs have to be fully dried.

Grebe (Y-O), 3, (4), S. A strong plant.

Green Howard (3W-GYY), 4, (4).

Green Island (2W-GWY), 4, (4).
Flowers of good substance held well
above foliage.

Gull (2W-GWW), 4, (4).

Hammoon (3W-Y), 3, (3).

Hawaii (4Y-R), 4, (4), S. Very robust
plant.

Hexameter (9W-YYR), 5, (4), P, S.
Similar to Cantabile.

Highland Wedding (2W-WWP), 4,
(3), S.

Hilford (2W-O), 3, (3).

Homage (2W-GWW), 4, (3).

Home Fires (2Y-R), 2, (4).

Hotspur (2W-R), 4, (4).

Ibis (6W-Y), 3, (3).

Ice Follies (2W-W), 4, (3), (FCC).
Very robust plant.

Imogen (2W-P), 4, (3). A good strong
colouring.

Inauguration (2Y-Y), 3, (3).

Infatuation (2W-GYP), 4, (3).

Innis Beg (2W-GWW), 4, (3).
Reliable cultivar that stands well.

Inverpolly (2W-W), 4, (3), SS.

Irish Light (2Y-R), 3, (3), SS.

Irish Minstrel (2W-Y), 4, (3), S, (FCC).

Irish Splendour (3W-R), 5, (3).

James Town (3W-GYY), 4 (3).

Jenny (6W-W), 2, (2), S, (AM).

Jet Fire (6Y-R), 2, (2), SS.

Jewel Song (2W-P), 4, (3), S.

N jonquilla (10Y-Y), 5, (1), P. Needs
well drained conditions in full sun.

Jumblie (6Y-O), 2, (1). Very similar to
Tête-à-Tête.

Karachi (2Y-YYR), 2, (3).

Karamudli (1W-Y), 3, (3), S.
Immaculate flower and sturdy plant.

Killeen (2Y-O), 3, (3), S. Almost
sunproof in most conditions.

Kilworth (2W-GRR), 4, (4), S.

Kimmeridge (3W-YYO), 3, (4), S.
Corona colour burns easily but
impressive perianth.

King Size (11Y-Y), 3, (4). Stands well
in spite of its size.

Kingbird (2Y-Y), 4, (4), S.

Knowhead (2W-W), 3, (3).

Lancaster (3W-GYO), 4, (4), S.

Lemon Beauty (11W-WWY), 3, (4).

Lemon Candy (2Y-WWY), 4, (4), SS.
Reverses well and of good form.

Lemonade (3Y-Y), 4, (4), S.

Liberty Light (2W-WWO), 2, (3).

Lichfield (3W-GYR), 4, (4).

Little Dancer (1W-Y), 3, (1).

Little Witch (6Y-Y), 1, (2). In some
conditions can appear a true
miniature, a colourful plant.

Loch Assynt (3W-GWO), 3, (4), SS.
A tall, strong grower.

Loch Brora (2W-O), 3, (3), S. An
unusual corona colour.

Loch Stac (2Y-R), 3, (3), S. A small
flower but stands well.

Loughanmore (1Y-Y), 4, (3), S.

Magnet (1W-Y), 3, (3). An old
cultivar but gives a good splash of
colour.

Mahmoud (3W-R), 4, (3).

Manly (4Y-O), 3, (4), S. Really a pale
orange, a double Golden Amber.

Martha Washington (8W-O), 3, (4), P.

Matador (8Y-GYO), 4, (3), P.

Matapan (3W-R), 3, (4).

Meavy (1W-W), 3, (3).

Mitylene (2W-Y), 3, (4).

Modest Maiden (2W-P), 4, (3).
Delicately coloured but sturdy plant.

Montego (3Y-YYO), 3, (3), S.
Colouring is variable.

Monterrico (4W-O), 4, (3), S.

Mount Hood (1W-W), 3, (3). Stands
well in most conditions.

Mrs R. O. Backhouse (2W-P), 4, (3).
The 'original' pink.

My Love (2W-Y), 3, (3), S.

Niveth (5W-W), 4, (3).

Notable (3W-GYO), 3, (3).

Ohio (2W-ORR), 6, (4), S.

Orangery (11W-POY), 3, (3).

Orion (2W-O), 4, (3), S.

Ormeau (2Y-Y), 3, (4), S. Strong
plant and a useful border plant.

Papua (4Y-Y), 3, (3), S.

Pasteline (2W-P), 3, (4).

Patrician (2Y-Y), 2, (4), S. A useful
early cultivar that stands well.

Paula Cottell (3W-WWY), 5 (1), S.

Pennine Way (1W-Y), 3, (3). Tends to
hang its head but looks well in
border.

Perimeter (3Y-YYR), 3, (4). Not very
strong yellow colouring but good
plant.

Pink Panther (2W-P), 3, (3), S. Very
deep colouring develops as flower
ages.

Pipe Major (2Y-R), 5, (3), S. Useful
later cultivar.

Pontresina (2W-Y), 4, (3), (AM).

Preamble (1W-Y), 2, (3).

Privateer (3W-O), 4, (3).

Prof. Einstein (2W-R), 3, (3).

Prologue (1W-Y), 1, (3).

Pueblo (7W-W), 4, (2), P. A creamy
white.

Pure Joy (2W-Y), 4, (4), S.

Queen Size (3W-Y), 4, (4), SS.

Rameses (2W-R), 4, (3), S.

Replete (4W-P), 3, (3), S. One of the
pure pink doubles.

Resplendent (2Y-R), 3, (4), S. Super
strong plant and almost sunproof.

Ringleader (2W-YYR), 3, (4), S.

Ringmaster (2Y-YYO), 3, (3), S.

Rio Rouge (2O-R), 3, (4). A most
unusual colour combination and
good plant.

Rippling Waters (5W-W), 4 (3). Very
floriferous bulbs.

Rockall (3W-R), 4, (3), S.

Romance (2W-P), 4, (3).

159

a) Colour coding in brackets,
   eg (4W-R)
b) Flowering season
   1 = very early season
   2 = early season
   3 = mid to main season
   4 = main season
   5 = late season
   6 = early summer
c) Height
   (1) = recognised miniature
   (2) = a plant generally up to 15in
         (38cm)
   (3) = a plant up to 20in (50cm)
   (4) = a plant over 20in (50cm)
d) Indication of significant perfume, P
e) Ability to produce show-quality
   blooms
   S = occasionally
   SS = fairly frequently
f) Awards after trial at Wisley
   (AM) = award of Merit
   (FCC) = First Class Certificate

N rupicola (10Y-Y), 3, (1). Needs well drained conditions, does well in alpine house.
Saberwing (5W-W), 3, (2), S. Strong plant and glistening flowers.
Salmon Spray (2W-P), 4, (3), SS.
Salmon Trout (2W-P), 4, (3).
Salome (2W-PPY), 5, (3), S. Yellowish rim always attracts attention.
Scarlet Gem (8Y-R), 3, (3), P.
Scio (2Y-Y), 3, (3), S.
Sea Green (9W-GGR), 6, (3), P, S. Old but outstanding late flowering cultivar.
Seraph (9W-GYR), 5, (3), P. S. A small bloom but good colour.
Silent Cheer (3W-YYR), 3, (3), S.
Silver Chimes (8W-W), 5, (3), P, S. Needs well drained conditions.
Silver Leopard (3W-WWY), 4, (4), S.
Simile (2W-GPP), 5, (3).
Slieveboy (1Y-Y), 4, (3).

Snowshill (2W-GWW), 4, (3).
Spun Honey (4Y-Y), 5, (3).
Saint Agnes (8W-O), 4, (3), P, (AM). Similar to Geranium but a neater flower.
Saint Anns (3W-R), 4, (4), S.
Stainless (2W-W), 4, (3), (AM).
Stourbridge (2Y-YOO), 3, (4), S. Flowers held well above foliage.
Stratosphere (7Y-O), 4, (4), P, S.
Suave (3Y-Y), 5, (6), S. Useful late flowering cultivar.
Suilven (3W-W), 4, (3). Good strong plant.
Sun Gleam (3Y-R), 3, (3).
Sunapee (3Y-YYR), 3, (3), S.
Suzy (7Y-O), 3, (4), P, S. Strong grower and good colour.
Sweetness (7Y-Y), 5, (4), P, S, (AM).
Tahiti (4Y-R), 3, (3), S. Makes an impressive splash of colour.
Tamar Fire (4Y-R), 3, (3), S. Very neat flower and stands well.
Tiritomba (11Y-O), 3, (3), S.
Toreador (3W-R), 4, (3).
Tresamble (5W-W), 5, (3).
Trevithian (7Y-Y), 2, (4), P. Stands well in most conditions.
Trousseau (1W-Y), 2, (3).
Tudor Love (2W-Y), 3, (3), S.
Tudor Minstrel (2W-Y), 3, (4), S, (AM).
Valdrome (11W-Y), 3, (3).
Vulcan (2Y-O), 2, (4), S, (FCC). Very strong plant and good flower.
W. P. Milner (1W-W), 2, (1).
Wedding Bell (2W-W), 2, (3).
Widgeon (2Y-PPY), 4, (3).
Willow Green (1W-Y), 2, (3). Strong plant and good for early display.
Woodland Prince (3W-Y), 3, (3).
Woodland Star (3W-R), 4, (3), S. Corona burns but still look impressive.
Yellow Cheerfulness (4Y-Y), 4, (3), P.

•10•
Daffodil Cycles

Daffodils as garden plants are ordered by two major cycles. The life or growth cycle starts with a viable seed and progresses through approximately five years. There are clearly identifiable incidents within this long time-scale which mark progress towards a mature plant capable of producing its own seed. Some fairly detailed appreciation of this seed-to-seed cycle of growth is of assistance to growers who want to be able to respond to the needs of the plant and maximise their pleasure from growing daffodils to their full potential.

The annual cycle can be based on incidents arising from flower through to next flower. This is a convenient approach for the average gardener or the keen exhibitor. It serves as a reminder of the key activities that must be undertaken to maintain the vigour of the plant and produce even better displays of colourful, enjoyable daffodils.

THE CYCLE OF GROWTH

All mature daffodil plants are described correctly as bulbous perennials. The characteristic bulb is effectively a storage mechanism which enables the plant to survive during the period of the year when climatic conditions are incompatible with the survival of foliage above the ground surface. It is often assumed that the daffodil bulb is a dormant organism between flowering periods as there are no external signs of development of the following season's plant. However, there is no sustained period of dormancy, for within the bulb various structures develop and become identifiable as the embryonic plant which begins its period of growth as soon as the conditions become favourable for macro growth.

Different species and cultivars of daffodil all have a cycle of growth based upon a periodicity of twelve months. The exact mechanisms of the various stimuli which regulate the cycle are not fully understood though it is clear that, in addition to genetically-dependent factors, temperature and light have great significance. Indeed, much practical experimentation has been undertaken to assess how these stimuli can best be manipulated to produce daffodil blooms over extended periods and satisfy the florists' demands for cut blooms. Temperature inevitably has a major influence on development of the embryo within the bulb, the foliage and the bloom. Light is essential for development and functioning of the foliage and in conjunction with temperature really regulates the rate of growth. Other stimuli, such as ethylene gas, are known to influence growth but the complexity of the mechanisms are such that they have little practical importance.

Individual daffodil cultivars readily reproduce themselves by vegetative means. The process of bulb division, explained in Chapter 2, which leads to the establishment of identical independent plants is generally a relatively slow process and is influenced by innate characteristics of the cultivar and by the cultural regime which is adopted. Some cultivars produce only limited numbers of bulbs by natural division, whereas others are relatively prolific. This vegetative multiplication limits the numbers of bulbs that can be produced in a given time and it cannot compete with the rate of multiplication achieved with subjects that can be reproduced from leaf or stem cuttings.

As the vast majority of daffodils are in effect garden hybrids, they cannot reproduce themselves by seeding. Each daffodil seed, except those from self-pollinated species, will be a unique new cultivar with some of the characteristics of each parent being genetically transmitted to each offspring. There is no real pattern or predictability as to which characteristics will be displayed in the offspring, but natural season of blooming, resistance to certain virus diseases, and vigour are known, from practical work, to be transmittable, whereas style of flower and colour are not clearly discernible in the first generation.

From seed to bulb All daffodils commence their existence as a seed and over a period of some five or six years gradually develop to mature plants capable of reproducing themselves by vegetative means. Daffodil seed looks very similar to that of the onion family, being shiny black and egg-shaped and about $1/16$ by $1/8$in (2 by 3mm). The seed structure is typical of a monocotyledon, having a single embryo leaf, and has a large solid endosperm, or reservoir of nutrients for the developing plant, occupying most of its interior, and a tiny embryo plant. Daffodil seeds are spread by the natural agencies of a distorting seedpod in combination with wind action and are distributed over a relatively small area. The seeds and young plants have to cope with the problem of naturally shallow planting and they have some ability to ensure that young bulbs are accommodated safely in the soil.

The seeds germinate after a period of some five to six months, dependent upon the conditions being sufficiently cool and moist. At germination the skin of the seed splits to allow a small radicle (root) to emerge and by gravitational stimulus to develop downwards into the soil. Subsequently, a single foliage leaf is initiated from the embryo and develops in an upward direction until it is clear of the soil and can commence functioning as a producer of food. Thus, in the early stages of growth the developing plant is absorbing its total requirements of nutrients from the endosperm, which gradually fades away. The radicle anchors the young plant into the soil and then begins to absorb water and nutrients to sustain the growth which has commenced. As the plant becomes less dependent upon the endosperm as its source of food, growth speeds up and two adventitious, or nutrient-seeking, roots are produced. These roots travel away from their point of origin and are more readily able to absorb nutrients from the soil and make the plant independent. The emergence of the adventitious roots effectively makes the radicle redundant and it gradually withers away.

At this stage it is possible to identify a tiny bulbous swelling at the base of the leaf which completely encloses the apical bud of the plant. The apical bud is effectively the point of initiation of the various identifiable structures that make up the complete plant. The single foliage leaf is green and semi-circular in section, and may attain a length of some 5 to 7in (13 to 18cm) dependent upon the supply of nutrients from the soil and the inherited characteristics of the cultivar. The adventitious roots will have extended to at least 5in (13cm) in length, though their direction of development will have been affected by the type of material through which they have travelled. Photosynthesis takes place within the leaf and the manufactured food is transported to the base of the leaf where it is stored as the scale leaves for the following season's growth.

Foliage die-back commences in early summer, the exact timing depending upon inherited stimuli and responses to temperatures, light intensity and water availability. As the leaf ceases to function it no longer directs additional food to the tiny bulb. At the same time the adventitious roots cease to function and become isolated from the bulb; however, before this takes place the stronger root has contracted in the area immediately below the bulb. This contraction drags the bulb deeper into the soil to where more favourable conditions exist for surviving the summer period. Eventually the leaf, roots and remnants of the seed are separated from the tiny bulb and decay into the soil. The bulb, which is usually about ½in (1cm) long, is now an independent plant protected from some extremes of the climatic conditions by the soil, but it is susceptible to attack from pests and diseases specific to the genus.

Development of the bulb During the summer and early autumn the tiny bulb will survive in the ground and will not display any outward signs of life. However, internally the apical bud will be developing the definable parts which will emerge as the following season's plant. Once the soil begins to cool down in the autumn, especially following rains, root action commences and some four to seven adventitious roots begin to extend into the surrounding soil. These roots are not all identical in size or strength and usually one is significantly larger than the others. Once the roots have become established and

163

capable of absorbing nutrients, a scale leaf begins to emerge from the neck of the bulb and when it is about ½in (1cm) long it splits to permit the true foliage leaves to break out and commence their passage to the surface of the soil. All of these activities absorb food from that stored in the tiny bulb, and it is only when the leaf has emerged from the soil and receives sufficient light that photosynthesis can begin and newly-manufactured food be available to sustain the relatively rapid growth of the leaves to their full potential of size.

In this second year of growth the young plant normally produces two foliage leaves which have the appearance of true daffodil leaves with a flattened cross-section. These leaves grow to some 7 or 8in (17 to 20cm) long and as they begin to reach this size they will be producing surplus food, above that required for their own growth, which is transported down to the bulb and stored within the scale leaves as a reserve upon which the plant will have to rely before the next growth of leaves can begin their photosynthesis. It is this storage process which gradually increases the size of the bulb by creating the scale leaves.

During this second year of growth the bulb increases its length and it becomes more cylindrical in shape. With reasonably favourable conditions a bulb about 1½in (4cm) long will be achieved. To accommodate this growth pattern, and to keep the bulb at an appropriate depth in the soil, one of the adventitious roots, usually the strongest, from early spring onwards contracts in the region of the base of the bulb and pulls the bulb further into the soil. Downward movement can be significantly in excess of ½in (1cm).

As late spring passes through to summer and the soil becomes drier and warmer, the two foliage leaves begin a process of isolation from the bulb and appear to die back. Very little of the substance of the leaves passes into the bulb as they desiccate and die. Subsequently the roots also cease to function and become separated from the bulb which is then ready to spend its period of isolation from its surrounding environment. Although appearing dormant the bulb is very much alive and subject to internal structural changes as the apical bud begins its definition and development ready for the next season of growth.

The pattern of growth in the third and fourth seasons closely follows that of the second year. With increasing size, the bulb is capable of providing the initial sustenance to a greater number of foliage leaves. A greater number of roots are also initiated compatible with increasing size of the base-plate. Damage to roots does sometimes occur and approximately 10 per cent (two or three roots) may be regenerated. Increased leaf and root production in turn enables greater subsequent build-up of the bulb to the stage at which the apical bud releases an embryo bloom and can sustain its development. Some bulbs will be large enough after four years to carry a flower, others may need one, two or even three additional years before commencing flower initiation.

Flower initiation Whilst the bulb is in its apparent phase of rest following its fourth season of growth the apical bud begins to define the parts of the flower, in addition to preparing the scale leaves for their period of growth. This process of development can commence within a week or two of the bulb becoming isolated from its redundant leaves and roots, and the rate of definition of all parts of the flower will depend to a large extent upon the genetic complexity of the particular cultivar. As the bud develops a number of clearly-defined stages have been identified:

1 The embryo initiates the leaves.
2 The enlarging embryo initiates the flower and then microscopically defines the various parts in the following sequence:
   — the initial for the spathe develops between the leaves;
   — the three outer perianth segments develop within the spathe;
   — the three inner perianth segments develop;
   — the three outer stamens are initiated;
   — the three inner stamens develop;
   — the three segments of the seedpod develop;
   — the circle of initials of the corona develop.

At this stage the full flower in miniature has been laid down and it gradually grows into an identifiable structure. The cooler conditions of late summer and early autumn encourage good development of the total bud within the bulb and by early autumn a dissected bulb will reveal a young growth perfect in all its detail.

Under favourable conditions all parts of the flower are formed in a period of about three weeks. In natural conditions, temperature variations due to the insulating effect of the soil are quite small and do not disturb the sequence of development or cause damage to the flower. However, excessive temperatures, for instance those experienced during any form of hot water treatment (see pages 33–4) carried out before all parts of the flower have been laid down, can disrupt the sequence and result in deformities that remain through to the following spring.

Throughout the autumn and winter the flower-bud continues to develop within the bulb. The bulb also begins to re-establish itself as a growing plant. The ring of adventitious roots, up to thirty in number, emerges from around the edge of the base-plate and firmly anchors the bulb into the soil. The sheath gradually elongates to bring the foliage leaves and the enclosed flower-bud to the surface. Growth is generally quite slow, about ⅛in (2mm) per week, and varies dependent upon the temperature of the soil as it impacts upon the growing tip. However, the leaves eventually emerge from the soil, where they respond quickly to the bright light which stabilises the chlorophyll to permit photosynthesis to begin.

The production of roots, leaves, flower-bud and stem is all undertaken at the expense of the food reserves of the bulb, which appears to lose weight. As photosynthesis takes place and water is absorbed by the roots, the essential requirements are available to sustain the rapid development of the plant. Only when the plant has fully developed is there any surplus of food from photosynthesis which can be diverted to rebuild the reserves within the bulb.

The stem bearing the flower-bud increases in length very rapidly once it has emerged above the soil. The bud is held vertically at the end of the stem, and the spathe and its enclosed flower gradually increase in size. Eventually the spathe stops growing and as its supplies of nutrients are cut off it begins to wither, to remain as a tissue of brown scales attached to the stem. Although the spathe ceases to grow the food is still transported to the flower which continues to expand until it ruptures the spathe. Coincident with this breaking from its protective layer the flower gradually tilts from a vertical position to near the horizontal. This curvature is induced by the combined effects of gravity and light so that the flower will face the direction of maximum light. The flower-bud develops in size and substance until the curvature of the three outermost perianth segments creates sufficient stresses to pull apart the interlocked barbs at their tips and the perianth springs back to its proper position to expose the corona. The complete flower continues to grow to maturity and the anthers continue to develop until they too open to expose the grains of pollen ready for fertilisation to take place.

Conditions of temperature and light will dictate how long the flower lasts before it shows signs of deterioration. As the perianth and corona begin to wither away the neck of the flower loses its curvature so that the ovary is again held vertically on the stem. If pollination has been achieved and the embryo seeds have been fertilised, the ovary will swell to give space for the seeds to develop. In natural conditions the majority of flowers will not have effected adequate pollination and, recognising that the ovary has no future use, the plant will cease providing food and it will wither away. In some cases the ovary will expand for ten to fifteen days, appearing as if it contains viable seed, before it then completely withers away — a false pregnancy, in effect.

At the same time as the various stages of flower development are taking place, major changes are occurring within the bulb. The stem has effectively ruptured the inner scales of the bulb and this initiates lateral division which will move to completion over the following two or three seasons. Additionally, a second, less mature, apical bud is initiated so that the original base-plate is now hosting two growing tips. The subsequent development of these two buds eventually leads to abscission of the base-plate and the establishment of two separate and identical plants. Thus, vegetative propagation is effected.

AN ANNUAL CYCLE

This can, for convenience, be taken as the period from flower to flower. We assume that this will be fifty-two weeks but due to vagaries of climate and seasonal variations it may vary between forty-nine and fifty-five weeks if a strict count is made.

Although the different cultivars flower at widely different times, each will maintain its own annual cycle. Thus, when a number of cultivars are being grown, slight adjustments to the timing of key events may have to be made for the grower's convenience. The extent of such compromises will depend upon many factors but provided good cultural and storage practices are being followed the resultant display of flowers should not be affected.

My own records show that I undertake a number of activities at the same time each season. The annual programme detailed below is based upon experience of a wide range of cultivars and, with appropriate allowances for variations in growth, should maintain healthy stock. In some seasons, strict adherence to dates may not comply with the signals from the plant. Carrying out one of the defined activities rather earlier than perfection would dictate is much less harmful than carrying it out a corresponding time later.

Week 1 The flowers are coming to the stage of full development, so cut them and exhibit them at a convenient show or take a few into the home. Whatever else you do, make sure that you enjoy the blooms.

Week 3 As the flowers fade, cut them from the stems and check that the foliage is not being rubbed or damaged in any way. Start a programme of foliar feeding and/or applying liquid fertilisers to help build up the bulbs.

Week 5 Keep checking that the foliage is not being damaged or flattened and add support as necessary. Watch the leaves for any signs of premature die-back and be prepared to apply a fungicide spray as a precautionary measure. Keep the area clear of competing weeds.

Week 9 Examine the leaves for the early signs of natural die-back and be ready to start lifting the bulbs when conditions are favourable. Take time to find your netting storage bags and clean the storage trays or racks.

Week 11 Brace yourself for lifting bulbs and as foliage dies back begin the operation. Carry out the preferred system of dipping of the bulbs and set them aside to dry off.

Week 12 As soon as the lifted bulbs are dry, carry out the first cleaning, paying particular attention to careful removal of roots and checking of base-plate.

Week 14 Tidy up beds and borders and burn the remnants of the foliage.

Week 16 Check over the bulbs again and carefully remove old tunics to create clean shiny bulbs that can be set aside ready for replanting. Make preparations for replanting and gather together all the tools, containers and composts/chemicals that will be required.

Week 18 Start replanting, giving suitable priority to pots and containers that will give early decorative displays. At this time one is permitted to dream of the fantastic blooms that will appear next spring.

Week 23 The whole planting operation should be completed, except for specially-prepared bulbs.

167

Week 26 Ensure that soil surfaces are clear of weeds, fallen leaves, stones and other debris. Consider the application of a herbicide to curtail emergence of further weeds.

Week 29 Plant a container of prepared bulbs for an early display. Repeat in weeks 31 and 33.

Week 30 Watch for signs of slug activity and apply a suitable treatment for their destruction.

Week 33 Bring pots or containers that are to be used for early, forced blooms into a suitable protected environment.

Week 38 Check beds and borders for the first signs of emerging shoots. Consider applying a light dressing of a balanced fertiliser.

Week 42 Lift pots of exhibition cultivars into a nice cool, airy environment. Assess the general conditions and decide upon any form of protection that may be necessary to keep the growth clean or to advance it slightly. Check all clumps of emerging shoots to ensure that their development is not being impeded or growing into foliage or twigs broken down by wind or snow.

Week 45 Start applying liquid fertilisers and get organised for any necessary tidying-up of foliage and flower shoots.

Week 46 Keep assessing the need for any watering and make sure pots and beds are not drying out. Adjust any ties that have been applied to keep pace with the development of the shoots. Have another blitz on the slug and insect population.

Week 47 If the blooms are to be protected make sure that everything is readily accessible.

Week 48 Get suitable protection positioned as necessary. Examine the developing flower-buds and start appreciating their potential beauty.

Week 49 Have a good look at all foliage and dig out any suspect plants showing major deformities.

Week 50 Make sure that the developing buds are not being impeded by their neighbours.

Week 51 Watch in amazement as the display of flowers comes to perfection.

Week 52 Enjoy the flowers in all of their splendour and get ready to start again from week 1.

The calendar of events shows a fairly full, if not quite weekly, programme. Daffodils can require some attention most weeks in the year and the more cultural techniques that are being practised the greater the number of related activities that will have to be slotted into the programme. Attention to detail does pay dividends and gives an even more spectacular display to grace any garden.

THE RHS CLASSIFICATION OF DAFFODILS

Since the first attempt to apply a standard system of classification to daffodils in 1896 there have been various moves to improve the provisions. Pressures for change have come from many sources, often from commercial operations trying to ensure that their cultivars are described correctly.

The system adopted by the Royal Horticultural Society in 1977 was a brave attempt to use computer technology as an adjunct to brief descriptions. By incorporating colour coding the revised system enables a fairly accurate mental picture of a particular cultivar to be built up. Of necessity, the colours identified for coding are limited and this is causing some problems as growers try to be more precise in their descriptions. For example, 'pink' conjures up certain conceptions of colour but the variety of shades is immense and ranges towards yellow, orange or red with, as yet, no definable boundary. Suggestions are being mooted for a greater number of colours to be used within the coding and there are arguments for and against any such change. Likewise, some of the definitions of Divisional characteristics may need refinement to reflect modifications that have been made progressively over the last twenty years. Whatever changes are ultimately made will no doubt be assimilated quickly by daffodil lovers everywhere. Meanwhile the present system is as detailed below.

1 The classification of a daffodil cultivar shall be based on the description and measurements submitted by the person registering the variety, or shall be the classification submitted by such person.
2 Colours applicable to the description of daffodil cultivars are abbreviated as follows:

W white or whitish   P pink
G green   O orange
Y yellow   R red

3 For the purpose of description, the daffodil flower shall be divided into perianth and corona.
4 The perianth shall be described by the letter or letters of the colour code most appropriate.
5 The corona shall be divided into three zones: an eye-zone, a mid-zone, and the edge or rim. Suitable coded colour descriptions shall describe these three zones, beginning with the eye-zone and extending to the rim.
6 The letter or letters of the colour code most accurately describing the perianth shall follow the Division designation.
7 The letters of the colour code most accurately describing the zones of the corona shall then follow, from the eye-zone to the rim, separated from the perianth letters by a hyphen. In Division 4, the letters of the colour code most accurately describing the admixture of the petals and petaloids replacing the corona shall follow in proper order, using 3, 2, or 1 colour codes as appropriate.
8 If the corona is substantially of a single colour, a single letter of the colour code shall describe it. Using these basic requirements, daffodils may be classified as follows:

Division 1: Trumpet daffodils of garden origin. Distinguishing characters: one flower to a stem; trumpet or corona as long or longer than the perianth segments.

Division 2: Long-cupped daffodils of garden origin. Distinguishing characters: one flower to a stem; cup or corona more than one-third, but less than equal to the length of the perianth segments.

Division 3: Short-cupped daffodils of garden origin. Distinguishing characters: one flower to a stem; cup or corona not more than one-third the length of the perianth segments.

Division 4: Double daffodils of garden origin. Distinguishing characters: double flowers.

Division 5: Triandus daffodils of garden origin. Distinguishing characters: characteristics of *Narcissus triandus* predominant.

Division 6: Cyclamineus daffodils of garden origin. Distinguishing characters: characteristics of *Narcissus cyclamineus* predominant.

Division 7: Jonquilla daffodils of garden origin. Distinguishing characters: characteristics of the *Narcissus jonquilla* group predominant.

Division 8: Tazetta daffodils of garden origin. Distinguishing characters: characteristics of the *Narcissus tazetta* group predominant.

Division 9: Poeticus daffodils of garden origin. Distinguishing characters: characteristics of the *Narcissus poeticus* group predominant.

Division 10: Species and wild forms and wild hybrids. All species and wild or reputedly wild forms and hybrids. Double forms of these varieties are included.

Division 11: Corona daffodils of garden origin. Distinguishing characters: corona split for at least one-third of its length.

Division 12: Miscellaneous daffodils. All daffodils not falling into any one of the foregoing Divisions.

AUTHOR'S NOTE

Cultivars registered prior to 1977 were not given colour codes by their raisers and have been slotted into the system by other individuals. Generally, the correct codes have been allocated, but some problems have arisen where cultivars show variation of colour due to climatic or cultural conditions.

For example, Drumboe has been coded as 2W-P but the intensity of colouring is delicate and often only shows as a rim of pink, so the code 2W-WWP may be more appropriate. Daydream has been coded as 2Y-W, but in some seasons and conditions it shows a distinct yellow colouring at the rim of the corona which could justify a code of 2Y-WWY.

Others are difficult to slot into the system, especially where the colours are of pastel tints or change throughout the development of the bloom. This absence of precision does not detract from the value of the system, but where show schedules specify required colours one must check whether judging will be as seen on the day or according to the allotted coding.

The provision for double daffodils allows the use of 1, 2 or 3 letters to describe the admix of petaloids. By common usage it is assumed that the majority of the dominant petaloids are the same colour as the perianth and it is only the contrast colour that is noted. For example, Gay Kybo has a whitish perianth and the centre of the flower contains a number of circles of whitish petaloids; interspersed amongst the latter are circles of much shorter orange petaloids. Technically, this should be coded as 4W-WWO, but by common usage this is abbreviated to 4W-O.

170

SYSTEMS FOR POINTING OF DAFFODILS

In any competitive situation criteria must be laid down against which assessments can be made. Pointing systems effectively define the good things and their relative contribution to the whole, but however good, or bad, the particular system, personal considerations come into play when the judge assesses the flower. Each judge should try to be consistent with his/her assessment under each defined attribute and should not allow personal preferences or prejudices to influence the outcome.

It is unfortunate that different pointing systems are thought to be necessary. The fact that they give different weightings to the various' attributes should not be too embarrassing if these are applied consistently. A good bloom should still perform well irrespective of the details of the system. The major pointing systems are summarised below.

THE DAFFODIL SOCIETY

Each flower is assessed against a standard and additional points are available for multi-bloom exhibits. This system clearly identifies the influence that presentation plays in multi-vase exhibits.

For a single stem		Points
Form and poise		3
Condition and texture		2
Colour		2
Size (for cultivar)		2
Stem		1
	Total:	10

For three blooms of one cultivar per vase an additional 2 points may be awarded for uniformity.

For multi-vase exhibits up to 10 points may additionally be awarded: for coverage of the Divisions and colour combinations within the definition of the class (up to 5 points); and for presentation of the total exhibit (up to 5 points).

The colour as defined in the registration details must be adhered to when staging in single-bloom classes. If a particular bloom is not as registered it can be shown in a multi-vase exhibit where it may be penalised on colour but will not be disqualified.

THE ROYAL HORTICULTURAL SOCIETY

Two scales of points are defined, dependent upon the number of flowers in each vase.

For single blooms		Points
Condition		4
Form		5
Colour		5
Size (for cultivar)		3
Texture		3
Poise		3
Stem		2
	Total:	25

For 3 or more stems		Points
Condition		4
Form		4
Colour		4
Size (for cultivar)		3
Texture		3
Poise		3
Stem		2
Uniformity		2
	Total:	25

Colour as displayed on the day will determine eligibility for single-bloom classes and this means that some cultivars can appear, and be successful, in more than one class.

THE AMERICAN DAFFODIL SOCIETY

In addition to defining the allocation of points the judging rules stipulate that before certain awards can be made each individual flower in an exhibit must score a minimum number of points. Such a criterion clearly ensures that special awards cannot be won by default with poor blooms.

For standard, single specimens, vases of 3 or 5 stems, and collections	*Points*
Condition	20
Form	20
Substance and texture	15
Colour	15
Poise	10
Stem	10
Size	10
Total:	100

For daffodils in pots (in growth)	*Points*
Exhibit as a whole:	40
Symmetry with uniform development (20)	
Floriferousness with good condition and substance (10)	
Condition and correctness of pot and label (10)	
Bloom and stem:	50
Same qualities in same relative importance as for cut specimens	
Foliage:	10
Condition (5)	
Colour (5)	
Total:	100

APPENDIX III
SOME SUPPLIERS OF MODERN DAFFODILS

Buying daffodil bulbs from a local nursery or supermarket may be convenient but the choice of cultivars will be limited to those which are believed to be popular. A much wider choice is available from specialist suppliers provided that orders are placed not later than midsummer (July in the UK). Their prices may be higher though ones or twos of particular cultivars can be purchased (most of the newer cultivars and exhibition favourites are priced per bulb). Bulbs should be stored in proper conditions once they are received, or planted immediately.

SPECIALISTS

The six specialist raisers below usually include new releases in their annual lists, as well as many of the established cultivars.

Mrs J. Abel Smith, Orchard House, Letty Green, Hertford, SG12 2NZ.

Ballydon Bulb Farm, Killinchy, Newtownards, Co Down, N Ireland, BT23 6QB.

Carncairn Daffodils Ltd, Carncairn Lodge, Broughshane, Ballymena, Co Antrim, N Ireland, BT43 7HF.

Clive Postles Daffodils, The Old Cottage, Purshall Green, Droitwich, Hereford and Worcester, WR9 0NL.

Rathowen Daffodils, Knowhead, Dergmoney, Omagh, Co Tyrone, N Ireland, BT78 1PN.

Grant E. Mitsch Novelty Daffodils, PO Box 218, Hubbard, Oregon 97032, USA.

The following eight specialists may include recent introductions but their lists are solely of daffodil cultivars which have been raised by other growers.

Constable Bulbs, 45 Weydon Hill Road, Farnham, Surrey, GU9 8NX.

Copford Bulbs, 1 Dorset Cottages, Birch Road, Copford, Colchester, Essex, CO6 1DR.

du Plessis Brothers, Marsh Farm, Landulph, Saltash, Cornwall, PL12 6NG.

Michael Jefferson-Brown Ltd, Weston Hills, Spalding, Lincs, PE12 6DQ.

Oakwood Daffodils, 2330 West Bertrand Road, Niles, Michigan 40120, USA.

Russell Graham, 4030 Eagle Crest Road NW, Salem, Oregon 97304, USA.

Gerard Knehans Jnr, Route One, Owensville, Missouri 65066, USA.

The Daffodil Mart, Rt 3, Box 794, Gloucester, Virginia 23061, USA.

GENERAL BULB SUPPLIERS

The following companies have general lists of bulbs though their ranges of daffodils are limited.

Avon Bulbs, Bathford, Bath, Avon, BA1 8ED.

Walter Blom & Son Ltd, Leavesden, Watford, Herts, WD2 7BH.

Broadleigh Gardens, Barr House, Bishops Hull, Taunton, Somerset, TA4 1AE (miniatures especially).

P. de Jager & Sons Ltd, The Nurseries, Marden, Kent, TN12 9BP.

Kelways Nurseries, Langport, Somerset, TA10 9SL.

van Tubergen, Oldfield Lane, Wisbech, Cambs, PE13 2RJ.

Wallace & Barr, The Nurseries, Marden, Kent, TN12 9BP.

The following nurseries have short but interesting lists of miniature types (including some species).

Rupert Bowlby, PO Box 156, Kingston-upon-Thames, Surrey, KT2 6AN.

P. J. & J. W. Christian, Pentre Cottages, Minera, Wrexham, Clwyd, LL11 3PD.

W. E. Th Ingwersen, Birch Farm Nursery, Cravetye, East Grinstead, Sussex, RN19 4LE.

Potterton & Martin, The Cottage Nursery, Moretown Road, Nettleton, Lincs, LN7 6HX.

McClure & Zimmerman, 1422W Thorndale, Chicago, Illinois 60660, USA.

Charles H. Mueller, River Road, New Hope, Pennsylvania 18938, USA.

Peter de Jager Bulbs, PO Box 2010, South Hamilton, Massachusetts 01982, USA.

ACKNOWLEDGEMENTS

Over many years my parents and family did much to develop my love of plants and without that initiation my interest in daffodils would never have emerged. I am also indebted to members of the Daffodil Society who have willingly passed on their knowledge and love of the genus; their fund of expertise has been invaluable.

The assistance of four individuals with converting my ideas into this book has been tremendous. My thanks go to: Jack Wood, who was instrumental in pulling the ideas out of me in the first place; John Davenport for faithfully recording the concepts in the photographs; Rosemary Wise for creating the line drawings from my roughs; and Sue Todd for converting my scrawl into a legible text with electronic devices. Many other people provided encouragement and material and I hope that my effort reflects their enthusiasm.

The major thanks must be to all breeders of daffodils for developing the genus to its present level of perfection with such enthusiasm that even higher standards are being pursued.

INDEX

175

176